The Yearbook of Courage and Serenity

Go, little book! From this my solitude;
I cast thee on the waters, — go thy ways:
And if, as I believe, thy vein be good,
The world will find thee after many days.
Be it with thee according to thy worth:
Go, little book! in faith I send thee forth.

ROBERT SOUTHEY

CELIA HADDON

The Yearbook of Courage and Serenity

BCA

LONDON · NEW YORK · SYDNEY · TORONTO

To
Estée Diamond

This edition published 1992 by BCA by arrangement with
MICHAEL JOSEPH LTD

Copyright © Celia Haddon 1992

Typeset in 11.5/12.5 Poliphilus

Colour origination by Anglia Graphics, Bedford
Printed and bound by Kyodo in Singapore

A CIP catalogue record for this book is available from the
British Library

CN 5764

A turning point in my life came when I first heard the prayer which opens this book. This prayer for courage and serenity has truly changed my life.

But the first time I first heard it, the word 'God' was hateful to my ears: the word itself had an aura of religiosity, self-righteousness, and condemnation. The god that I believed in (though I told myself I was an atheist) was a tyrant bent on torturing mankind. He was my moral inferior who would doom me and those I loved to Hell.

Yet I needed a spiritual programme; I needed a sense of meaning in my life; I needed a loving God. That false unloving god stood in the way of the true God of love. It has taken me years to root that cruel and demanding presence out of my spiritual life.

Sometimes that false god comes back into my mind and fills me with self-condemnation and fear. For a time I may have to set aside all thoughts of a Higher Power and even stop praying, in order to keep that tyrant out of my mind. If I do this calmly, eventually I find my way back to the God which is love, or perhaps the God of love finds the way back to me.

If any of you, who are reading this book, find the word 'God' difficult or worrying, I beg you simply to substitute a word like 'love', or give it any meaning you choose, or just do not bother with giving it a meaning. There is no need to define God. Experiencing a life with God is the aim – not defining, understanding or talking about it.

I have used some of the paintings of my mother, Joyce Haddon, to illustrate this book. She explores in paint what I try to explore in words.

Celia Haddon

JANUARY

God give us the grace to accept with serenity the things that
  cannot be changed;
Courage to change the things that should be changed;
And the wisdom to distinguish the one from the other.

*I was introduced to this prayer, written by a Protestant minister,
Reinhold Niebuhr, when I needed to make a drastic change in my life. I
still use it regularly. It has been so important to me that it provides the
theme of this book. Both acceptance and change are difficult for me. The
things I must accept with serenity include other people and many of the
events that happen around me. I must also accept, and learn to love,
myself. I need courage just to look inwards. When I dare to examine
my true self, good and bad, then I may find that I want to change some
of my behaviour and some of my thought patterns.*

Since to be loved endures,
To love is wise:
Earth hath no good but yours,
Brave, joyful eyes:

Earth hath no sin but thine,
Dull eye of scorn:
O'er thee the sun doth pine
And angels mourn.

ROBERT BRIDGES

JANUARY 3   It seems as if the day was not wholly profane in which we have given heed to some natural object. The fall of snowflakes in a still air, preserving to each crystal its perfect form; the blowing of sleet over a wide sheet of water, and over plains ... the crackling of hemlock in the flames; or of pine logs, which yield glory to the walls and faces in the sitting room, – these are the music and pictures of the most ancient religion.

Like Ralph Waldo Emerson, I find something serene in the impersonal beauty of nature. It is just there, whether I notice it or not. When I do notice it during the day, I am less self-obsessed.

JANUARY 4
He said not:
'Thou shalt not be tempested;
Thou shalt not be travailed:
Thou shalt not be afflicted.'
But He said:
'Thou shalt not be overcome.'

Heartening words from the medieval Dame Julian of Norwich.

JANUARY

Nothing would be done at all if a man waited until he could do it so well that no one would find fault with it.

JANUARY 5

JOHN HENRY NEWMAN

JANUARY 6

Today is the feast of the three wise men who followed a star until they came to a newly born baby. John Greenleaf Whittier's verse celebrates the wisdom of seeing what we can learn from a child or from the spontaneous and childlike part of our inner selves.

> We need love's tender lessons taught
> As only weakness can;
> God hath His small interpreters;
> The child must teach the man.

JANUARY 7

A great deal of talent is lost in the world for want of a little courage. Every day sends to their graves obscure men whom timidity prevented from making a first effort; who, if they could have been induced to begin, would in all probability have gone great lengths in the career of fame. The fact is, that to do anything in the world worth doing, we must not stand back shivering and thinking of the cold and danger but jump in and scramble through as well as we can.

SYDNEY SMITH

JANUARY 8

> My business is not to remake myself,
> But make the absolute best of what God made.

ROBERT BROWNING

JANUARY 9

If winter bellow from the north,
Soon the sweet spring comes dancing forth,
And nature laughs again.

What if thine heaven be overcast?
The dark appearance will not last;
Expect a brighter sky.

William Cowper tells us that winter heralds spring. In the same way I can accept sad times, knowing that they will not last for ever.

JANUARY 10

As God loveth a cheerful giver, so He also loveth a cheerful taker, who takes hold on His gifts with a glad heart.

JOHN DONNE

JANUARY 11

Having something to work at (and it is not always a paid job) is essential for our well-being. So says James Russell Lowell.

No man is born into the world, whose work
Is not born with him: there is always work,
And tools to work withal, for those who will.

JANUARY 12

Courage and perseverance have a magical talisman, before which difficulties disappear and obstacles vanish into air.

I like this sentence by the American statesman, John Quincy Adams. Courage is not always within my grasp but perseverance I can usually achieve. It can step in and help me when my courage seems to fail.

I hear and behold God in every object, yet understand God
   not in the least,
Nor do I understand who there can be more wonderful than
   myself.

Why should I wish to see God better than this day?
I see something of God each hour of the twenty-four, and each
   moment then,
In the faces of men and women I see God and in my own
   face in the glass.

*Walt Whitman conveys the idea that God is seen through people. I
must stop trying to puzzle it out and just accept God in each day.*

To talk and laugh with mutual
concessions, to read pleasant books;
to jest and to be solemn, to
dissent from each other without
offence, to teach one another
somewhat, or somewhat to
learn – to expect those
absent with impatience and
embrace their return with
joy.

*This definition of friendship
was written by St Augustine.
Friends are those who help me
renew my courage when life gets
me down.*

JANUARY 15

In one of my favourite novels, The Sword in the Stone *by T.H.White, the magician Merlin gives this remedy for melancholy.*

The best thing for being sad is to learn something. That is the only thing that never fails. You may grow old and trembling in your anatomies, you may lie awake at night listening to the disorder of your veins, you may miss your only love, you may see the world about you devastated by evil lunatics, or know your honour trampled in the sewers of baser minds. There is only one thing for it then – to learn ... That is the only thing which the mind can never exhaust, never alienate, never be tortured by, never fear or distrust, and never dream of regretting.

JANUARY 16

I am but one, but I am one.
I cannot do everything; but I can do something.
What I can do, I ought to do.
What I ought to do, by the grace of God, I will do.
Lord, what will you have me do?

The motto of the American Order of the Daughters of the King.

JANUARY

JANUARY 17

In the book of Ecclesiasticus there is this passage about the mysterious beauty of snow and frost. May I notice this miracle.

As birds flying, He scattereth the snow, and the falling down thereof is as the lighting of grasshoppers:

The eye marvelleth at the beauty of the whiteness thereof, and the heart is astonished at the raining of it.

The hoarfrost also as salt he poureth on the earth, and being congealed it lieth on the top of sharp stakes.

JANUARY 18

It is perhaps better to make the mistakes of facing life than to make the mistakes of running away from life.

HAVELOCK ELLIS

JANUARY 19

How small of all that human hearts endure,
That part which laws or kings can cause or cure.
Still to ourselves in every place consigned,
Our own felicity we make or find.

SAMUEL JOHNSON

JANUARY 20

When you find yourself, as I dare say you sometimes do, overpowered as it were by melancholy, the best way is to go out, and do something kind to somebody or other. Writing, too, I have known in many cases a very great relief ... I fancy the best way would be to write on till one was a little unburthened, and then put one's confessions in the fire.

JOHN KEBLE

JANUARY 21

We never know how high we are
Till we are asked to rise,
And then if we are true to plan
Our statures touch the skies —

The heroism we recite
Would be a normal thing
Did not ourselves the cubits warp
For fear to be a king

EMILY DICKINSON

JANUARY 22

If I am not for myself, who is for me? But if I am only for myself what am I? And if not now, when?

RABBI HILLEL

JANUARY 23

If things of sight such heavens be,
What heavens are those we cannot see?

ANDREW MARVELL

JANUARY 24

Barbara Bush, the wife of the American President, had this to say in one of her speeches. In the busy rush of daily life, it is sometimes difficult to remember what really matters. Many of our concerns and our obsessions simply aren't that important.

At the end of your life, you will never regret not having passed one more test, not winning one more verdict, or not closing one more deal. You will regret time not spent with a husband, a child, a friend or a parent.

JANUARY

On his birthday in 1793 Robert Burns heard a thrush singing.

Sing on, sweet thrush, upon the leafless bough;
Sing on, sweet bird, I listen to thy strain:
See agèd winter, 'mid his surly reign,
At thy blithe carol clears his furrowed brow.

So in lone poverty's dominion drear
Sits meek content with light unanxious heart,
Welcomes the rapid moments, bids them part,
Nor asks if they bring aught to hope or fear.

I thank thee, Author of this opening day!
Thou whose bright sun now gilds the orient
    skies!
Riches denied, thy boon was purer joys,
What wealth could never give nor take away!

If a man is not thinking about
himself, he is himself.

WILLIAM MORRIS

JANUARY 27

Driving between Norwich and Kings Lynn I took a turning off ... and quite unexpectedly, in a little street near by, in a small outhouse the size of a shed, there was a shrine to the almost forgotten Saxon saint, Walston. He was the son of a wealthy family. One day he left his secure background to go wherever God led him. God led him, his way indicated by oxen, not far away to an ordinary farm, which wasn't very dramatic. Walston became a farmhand there, an ordinary agricultural labourer as he remained throughout his life, healing humans and animals without making any song and dance about it. He was the antidote to the search for status and over-concentration on worldly success. He was a non-celebrity saint.

RABBI LIONEL BLUE

JANUARY 28

Love lights the sun: love through the dark
Lights the moon's evanescent arc:
Same love lights up the glow-worm's spark.

CHRISTINA ROSSETTI

One should take good care not to grow too wise for so great a pleasure of life as laughter.

JANUARY 29

JOSEPH ADDISON

Many gift shops now sell verses printed on plastic wallet cards. Just doggerel they may be, but some, like this one, I really enjoy.

JANUARY 30

When things go wrong as they sometimes will,
When the road you're trudging seems all uphill,
When the funds are low and the debts are high,
And you want to smile but you have to sigh,
When care is pressing you down a bit,
Rest, if you must, but don't you quit.
Life is queer with its twists and turns,
As every one of us sometimes learns,
And many a failure turns about
When he might have won had he stuck it out ...
And you never can tell how close you are –
It may be near when it seems far.
So stick to the fight when you're hardest hit:
It's when things seem worst you must not quit.

When the body is kept bustling about without stop, it becomes fatigued. When the mind is overworked without stop, it becomes worried, and worry causes exhaustion. The nature of water is that it becomes clear when left alone and becomes still when undisturbed. It is the symbol of heavenly virtue.

JANUARY 31

CHUANGTSE

FEBRUARY

I asked for strength that I might achieve;
I was made weak that I might learn humbly to obey.
I asked for health that I might do greater things;
I was given infirmity that I might do better things.
I asked for riches that I might be happy;
I was given poverty that I might be wise.
I asked for power that I might have the praise of men;
I was given weakness that I might feel the need of God.
I asked for all things that I might enjoy life;
I was given life that I might enjoy all things.
I got nothing that I had asked for,
But everything that I had hoped for.
Almost despite myself my unspoken prayers were answered;
I am, among all men, most richly blessed.

AN UNKNOWN CONFEDERATE SOLDIER

Today is the old feast of Candlemas. I sometimes recapture my serenity by lighting a candle and sitting quietly within its light. Charles Lamb, the kindly essayist, praised candlelight like this.

Hail, candlelight! without disparagement to sun or moon, the kindliest luminary of the three – mild viceroy of the moon! We love to read, talk, sit silent, eat, drink, sleep, by candlelight. They are everybody's sun and moon. This is our peculiar and household planet.

FEBRUARY 3   The theologian dreams of a God sitting above the clouds among the cherubim; but we enthrone him upon the wings of birds, on the petals of flowers, on the faces of our friends, and upon whatever we most delight in of all that lives upon the earth. We then can not only love Him, but we can do that without which love has neither power nor sweetness, we can express our love and have it expressed to us in return. And this is not in the uprearing of stone temples, nor yet in the cleansing of our hearts, but in the caress bestowed upon horse and dog, and kisses upon the lips of those we love.

SAMUEL BUTLER

FEBRUARY 4   *The writer, Denys Watkins-Pitchford, prefaced all his books with these words which he found on an old gravestone.*

The wonder of the world,
The beauty and the power,
The shapes of things,
Their colours, lights, and shades,
These I saw.
Look ye also while life lasts.

FEBRUARY

What is invisible to the eyes can be seen with the heart.

MOTTO FROM A SCHOOL FOR THE DISABLED

John Clare, a farmworker and also a great poet, wrote these verses,
'On Seeing Some Moss in Flower Early in Spring'. He had an eye
for the small things of nature and saw the joy in them.

> This common moss so hid from view
> To heedless crowd unknown,
> By nature made as happy too,
> Finds seasons of its own.
>
> It peeps among the fallen leaves
> On every stoven grows:
> Sufficient sun its shade receives
> And so it buds and blows.
>
> Thus common things in every place
> Their pleasing lessons give.
> They teach my heart life's good to trace
> And learn me how to live.
>
> They feed my heart with one consent
> That humble hope and fear,
> That quiet peace and calm content,
> Are blessings everywhere.

Respect yourself. The rest will follow.

PYTHAGORAS

FEBRUARY 8

The good we do today becomes
The happiness of tomorrow.

HINDU PROVERB

FEBRUARY 9

Of all the heavenly gifts, that mortal men commend,
What trusty treasure in the world can countervail a
    friend?
What sweeter solace shall befall, than one to find
Upon whose breast thou may'st repose the secrets of thy
    mind?

NICHOLAS GRIMALD

FEBRUARY 10

To shirk pain, bearable pain, altogether is not only to be less
real than one might have been: it is to isolate oneself from the
common lot of pain, from the pain of humanity and the world.
It is to blunt or cut off or withdraw one's antennae; it is to play
only such notes as one chooses in the universal symphony,
which is a symphony of suffering as well as of joy.

*This passage by Victor Gollancz reminds me that I cannot escape pain.
Evading pain brings only difficulties and dishonesties.*

FEBRUARY 11

The talent God doth give, must be employed.
His own with vantage he must have again:
All parts and faculties were made for use;
The God of knowledge nothing gave in vain.

A seventeenth-century woman poet, Rachel Speght, wrote this.

Put your hands to work and your heart to God. Do all your work as though you had a thousand years to live, and as you would if you knew you must die tomorrow.

This is a saying of Ann Lee, founder of the Shaker movement. There is a pleasure, a great pleasure, in doing things properly.

Flowers are an inspiration. Hartley Coleridge wrote of snowdrops and the hope they bring even to the heart that is almost hopeless.

One month is past, another is begun,
Since merry bells rang out the dying
        year,
And buds of rarest green began to peer,
As if impatient for a warmer sun;
And though the distant hills are bleak
        and dun,
The virgin snowdrop, like a lambent
        fire,
Pierces the cold earth with its green-
        streaked spire
And in dark woods, the wandering little
        one
May find a primrose. Thus the better
        mind
Puts forth some flowers, escaped from
        paradise,
Though faith be dim as faintest wintry
        skies.

FEBRUARY 14

Today birds choose their mates and sing their courtship from trees, bushes and city buildings. John Donne celebrates this day.

Hail, Bishop Valentine,
   whose day this is:
All the air is thy diocese,
And all the chirping
   choristers
And other birds are thy
   parishioners:
Thou marriest every year
The lyric lark and the grave
   whispering dove,
The sparrow that neglects his
   life for love,
The household bird with the red stomacher.

FEBRUARY 15

Let us no longer think so much about punishing, blaming and improving! We shall seldom be able to alter an individual. Let us rather see to it that our own influence on all that is to come outweighs his influence! Let us not struggle in direct conflict! – all blaming, punishing and desire to improve comes under this category. Let us give to our pattern more shining colours! Let us obscure the other by our light.

FRIEDRICH NIETZCHE

A disciple asked the Baal Shem: 'Why is it that one who clings to God and knows he is close to him, sometimes experiences a sense of interruption and remoteness?' The Baal Shem explained: 'When a father sets out to teach his little son to walk, he stands in front of him and holds his two hands on either side of the child, so that he cannot fall, and the boy goes toward his father between his father's hands. But the moment he is close to his father, he moves away a little and holds his hands farther apart, and he does this over and over, so that the child may learn to walk.'

MARTIN BUBER

This world's no blot for us,
Nor blank; it means intensely, and means good.

ROBERT BROWNING

In the sermons of Jeremy Taylor is this beautiful passage about the thaw. I would like my own heart to come back to life this way.

So have I seen the sun kiss the frozen earth which was bound up with the images of death and the colder breath of the north; and then the waters break from their enclosures, and melt with joy, and run in useful channels; and the flies to rise again from their little graves in walls and dance awhile in the air, to tell that there is joy within and the great mother of creatures will open the stock of her new refreshment, become useful to mankind, and sing praises to her Redeemer.

FEBRUARY 19   The law of worthy life is fundamentally the law of strife. It is only through labour and painful effort, by grim energy and resolute courage, that we move on to better things.

There is no inner change, says Theodore Roosevelt, without effort.

FEBRUARY 20   *This is my favourite passage from the revised version of the Old Testament. Isaiah describes God's love. I read this as a pledge that God means me to be who I am, and that His care can transform me.*

Fear not: for I have redeemed thee: I have called thee by thy name: thou art mine.
   When thou passest through the waters, I will be with thee; And through the rivers, they shall not overflow thee;
   When thou walkest through the fire, thou shalt not be burned; Neither shall the flame kindle upon thee ...
   Since thou hast been precious in my sight, and honourable, and I have loved thee; ...
   Fear not; for I am with thee.

FEBRUARY 21   I have told you of the man who always put on his spectacles when about to eat cherries, in order that the fruit might look larger and more tempting. In like manner I always make the most of my enjoyments, and, though I do not cast my eyes away from troubles, I pack them into as small a compass as I can.

ROBERT SOUTHEY

These verses by Charles Cotton are about being content. He uses the *old word 'contentation' where we would say 'contentment'.*

> 'Tis contentation that alone
> Can make us happy here below,
> And when this little life is gone
> Will lift us up to Heaven too.

> A very little satisfied
> And honest and a grateful heart,
> And who would more than will suffice,
> Does covet more than is his part.

There is a cartoon book by Suzy Becker, titled All I Need To Know I Learned From My Cat. *Here are some of the things her cat taught her. I really like them. We can all learn them by watching cats.*

Be curious.
Make the world your playground.
Recognise the toy in everything.
Depend on others without losing
   your independence.

FEBRUARY 24 Father in heaven! When the thought of thee wakes in our hearts, let it not awaken like a frightened bird that flies about in dismay, but like a child waking from its sleep with a heavenly smile.

There's great wisdom in these words by Soren Kierkegaard. We can trust God to be there for us, waiting with loving acceptance.

FEBRUARY 25

Give all to love;
Obey thy heart;
Friends, kindred, days,
Estate, good fame,
Plans, credit and the Muse –
Nothing refuse.

'Tis a brave master;
Let it have scope:
Follow it utterly,
Hope beyond hope.

Be brave enough to do the loving thing, says Ralph Waldo Emerson.

Spirituality is the basis and foundation of human life. It must underlie everything. To put it briefly, man is a spiritual being, and the proper work of his mind is to interpret the world according to his higher nature.

Everybody has some kind of spirituality, according to Robert Bridges. Most people are happier with a meaning for their life. By caring for my inner spirit, I give myself some inner serenity.

FEBRUARY 26

> You must not only aim aright,
> But draw the bow with all your might.

HENRY DAVID THOREAU

FEBRUARY 27

A new life begins for us with every second. Let us go forward joyously to meet it. We must press on, whether we will or no, and we shall walk better with our eyes before us than with them ever cast behind.

The writer Jerome K. Jerome reminds us that we can always start anew, putting the past behind us and living in the present.

FEBRUARY 28

This little verse, found in an old house on a ceiling dial, offers the right thought for the extra day which comes every four years.

FEBRUARY 29

> See the little daystar moving,
> Life and time are worth improving,
> Seize the moments, while they stay,
> Seize and use them,
> Lest you lose them,
> And lament the wasted day.

MARCH

I cannot ope mine eyes,
But Thou art ready there to catch
My morning soul, and sacrifice ...
Teach me Thy love to know;
That this new light, which now I see,
May both the work and Workman show:
Then by a sunbeam I will climb to Thee.

*For the morning of St David's Day some lines on waking up by
George Herbert, the Welsh poet. I particularly love the last line.*

We say abstractly: 'I mean to enjoy poetry, and to absorb a lot
of it, of course. I fully intend to keep up my love of music, to
read the books that shall give new turns to the thought of my
time, to keep my higher spiritual side alive, etc.' But we do not
attack these things concretely, and we do not begin today. We
forget that every good that is worth possessing must be paid for
in strokes of daily effort. We postpone and postpone, until those
smiling possibilities are dead. Whereas ten minutes a day of
poetry, of spiritual reading or meditation, and an hour or two a
week at music, pictures, or philosophy, provided we began now
and suffered no remission, would infallibly give us in due time
the fullness of all we desire.

WILLIAM JAMES

MARCH 3 The principles of mental hygiene are as follows. Can you let unimportant things go? Can you learn not to depend on others but to seek it in yourself? Can you be innocent like a new-born child? The baby cries all day and yet his voice never becomes hoarse; that is because he has not lost nature's harmony. The baby clenches his hands all day without holding anything; that is because he is following his original character. The baby looks at things all day without winking; that is because his eyes are not focused on any particular object.

The message of Lao Tse, a Taoist sage, is that we should be living less self-consciously, in harmony with the world. If I try to accept what happens, I need not be so busy in judging whether it is right or wrong, lucky or unlucky. We should just accept.

MARCH 4 The innocent brightness of a new born day
Is lovely yet.

WILLIAM WORDSWORTH

Wait on the Lord: Be strong, and he shall
strengthen thine heart: wait, I say on the Lord.

PSALM 27

A friend of mine found this verse carved on a stone step in the Dublin Botanic Gardens forty years ago. Perhaps it is still there.

A friendly look,
A kindly smile,
One good act,
And life's worthwhile.

There is no wealth but life. Life, including all its powers of love, of joy, and of admiration. That country is the richest which nourishes the greatest number of noble and happy human beings.

In this remark by John Ruskin what makes me pause is the word 'admiration'. To admire a picture, a landscape, a flower, a deed or a person, is to enrich and inspire ourselves. Maybe we could say it is happier to admire than to be admired: we benefit more.

Friendship relieveth man's necessity,
Friendship comforteth man's adversity,
Friendship augmenteth man's prosperity.

An anonymous poet wrote these lines in a charming anthology more than four centuries ago, entitled The Paradise of Dainty Devices. *He signed them 'F.K.' They struck me as worth passing on.*

MARCH 9   The artist in each of us needs to be let out of the closet. It deserves to be shared, to be wondered at, to be celebrated, and to be criticized. This letting out may take the form of storytelling and conversing; doing carpentry or repairs; writing or dancing; painting or parenting; singing or clowning. If what is let out truly flowers from our depths, then it is flowing from God's depths too.

MATTHEW FOX

MARCH 10

Not what we did, shall be the test,
When act and will are done,
But what our Lord infers we would,
Had we diviner been.

EMILY DICKINSON

MARCH 11   Whatever falls to thee to do, that perform as much as thou canst faithfully and diligently; but be not too anxious as to how it may turn out.

This comes from the writings of Mary Ward, a seventeenth century Catholic who tried to found a women's equivalent of the Jesuits. We are responsible for the effort, not the results.

MARCH 12

Our doubts are traitors
And make us lose the good we oft might win,
By fearing to attempt.

WILLIAM SHAKESPEARE

MARCH

MARCH 13

Never a day passes but men and women of no great note do
great deeds, speak great words, and suffer noble sorrows.

A reminder by Charles Reade that we can find courage and serenity in
ordinary people — if we look for the best in them.

MARCH 14

Let me not deem that I was made in vain,
Or that my being was an accident,
Which fate, in working its sublime intent,
Not wished to be, to hinder would not deign.
Each drop uncounted in a storm of rain
Hath its own mission, and is duly sent
To its own leaf or blade; not idly spent
'Mid myriad dimples on the shipless main.
The very shadow of an insect's wing,
For which the violet cared not, while it stayed,
Yet felt the lighter for its vanishing,
Proved that the sun was shining by its shade.

I find this poem by Hartley Coleridge moving. Each
person is precious, created for a purpose, though we do
not know what it is.

MARCH 15   Thou hearest the nightingale begin the song of spring:
The lark sitting upon his earthy bed; just as the morn
Appears; listens silent; then springing from the waving
   cornfield! loud
He leads the choir of day! trill, trill, trill, trill,
Mounting upon the wings of light into the great expanse;
Re-echoing against the lovely blue and shining heavenly
   shell:
His little throat labours with inspiration; every feather
On throat and breast and wings vibrates the effluence divine.
All Nature listens silent to him, and the awful sun
Stands still upon the mountain looking at this little bird.

William Blake was a visionary, seeing heaven all around us.

MARCH 16   If you love something, let it go. If it returns to you, it's yours. If
it doesn't, it never was.

ANONYMOUS

MARCH

For St Patrick's Day, an Irish blessing to a friend. What I like about this blessing is that it is a modest request: it doesn't ask too much.

> May there always be work for your hands to do;
> May your purse always hold a coin or two;
> May the sun always shine on your windowpane;
> May a rainbow be certain to follow each rain;
> May the hand of a friend always be near you;
> May God fill your heart with gladness to cheer you.

MARCH 18

> We charge no soul with more than it can bear.
>
> THE KORAN

MARCH 19

> I say that man was made to grow, not stop;
> That help he needed once, and needs no more,
> Having grown but an inch by, is withdrawn;
> For he hath new needs, and new helps to these...
> Since all things suffer change save God the Truth,
> Man apprehends Him newly at each stage.

In Robert Browning's poems there are many lines about inner growth. The wisdom in this extract lies in the thought that we do not stop growing. There is no arriving, only journeying. If we do not stay open to change, we risk becoming rigid, only half alive.

MARCH 20

A man may fulfil the object of his existence by asking a question he cannot answer, and attempting a task he cannot achieve.

OLIVER WENDELL HOLMES

MARCH 21   Think fairly; love widely; witness humbly; build bravely.

This is one of those anonymous pieces of wisdom, passed from person to person, kept in wallets and purses, because somehow they speak to the human condition — truly popular philosophy.

MARCH 22   *I am sometimes tortured by self-hatred, disguised as a kind of religiosity. These words by John Henry Newman are a corrective.*

That repentance is not real which has not love in it; that self-chastisement is not acceptable which is not sweetened by faith and cheerfulness. We must live in sunshine, even when in sorrow.

MARCH 23   Earth gets its price for what earth gives us;
The beggar is taxed for a corner to die in,
The priest has his fee who comes and shrives us,
We bargain for the graves we lie in;
At the devil's booth all things are sold,
Each ounce of dross costs its ounce of gold;
For a cap and bells our lives we pay,
Bubbles we buy with a whole soul's tasking:
'Tis heaven alone that is given away,
'Tis only God may be had for the asking.

JAMES RUSSELL LOWELL

MARCH 24   Life is not just a problem to be solved. It is a path to be explored.

AUTHOR UNKNOWN

Be a Columbus to whole new continents and worlds within you, opening new channels, not of trade but of thought.

HENRY DAVID THOREAU

This delightful poem was written at the court of Henry VIII by the poet and composer, William Cornyshe, who died in 1523.

Pleasure it is
To hear, iwis,
The birdès sing.
The deer in the dale,
The sheep in the vale,
The corn springing;
God's purveyance
For sustenance
It is for man.
Then we will always
To Him give praise.

MARCH 27

Through what fierce incarnations, furled
In fire and darkness, did I go,
'Ere I was worthy in the world
To see a dandelion grow?

This verse by G.K. Chesterton pleases me because I have always thought the dandelion a magnificent flower. Ignored as a weed, it glows with a startling glory in hedges and on urban wasteland.

MARCH 28

If we consider what persons have stimulated and profited us, we shall perceive the superiority of the spontaneous or intuitive principle over the arithmetical or logical. In every man's mind some images, words, and facts remain, without effort on his part to imprint them, which others forget, and afterwards these illustrate to him important laws. All our progress is an unfolding. Trust the instinct to the end, though you can render no reason. We are all wise. It is long ere we discover how rich we are.

These sentences from an essay by Ralph Waldo Emerson tell us we should live by the heart. Man does not live by intellect alone.

If all were rain and never sun,
No bow could span the hill;
If all were sun and never rain,
There'd be no rainbow still.

CHRISTINA ROSSETTI

We are constantly tempted to make God in our own image, to divinize our narrowness and self-importance and then call it the will of God. God is mystery, a beckoning word, and He calls us out beyond our narrowness. Our one security is that He is, not in our formulation of how He is. Because we are made in God's image, therefore we share in His mystery. If we all have different finger-prints, it is not so surprising that we should also have our own unique way of knowing and understanding God. We are all making the same journey, but the route is different for each and we have to discover it in freedom.

This passage comes from God of Surprises, *by Gerard W. Hughes, a book which meant a great deal to me in my search for the loving real God, rather than the judgemental God of man-made religion.*

This two-line poem by Walt Whitman, entitled 'To You', is about the needless barriers between human beings. If we trusted each other more, perhaps we could talk more freely to each other.

Stranger, if you passing meet me and desire to speak to
    me, why should you not speak to me?
And why should I not speak to you?

APRIL

APRIL 1

The meadows they are emerald green;
The river sparkles with the light;
Like snowstorms are the orchard seen;
The fields are with daisies white;
The buttercups are buds of green
That by and by are flowers of gold;
The fields look warm, the air serene
And all is lovely to behold.

'Tis spring, the April of the year,
The holiday of birds and flowers.
Some build e'er yet the leaves appear,
While others wait for safer hours:
Hid in green leaves that shun the shower,
They're safe and happy all along;
The meanest weed now finds a flower;
The simplest bird will learn a song.

This poem by John Clare is about the country, but even in towns we can see spring's beauty in parks and listen to sparrows and pigeons. I find inner turmoil quietens when I notice such things.

APRIL 2

Beloved, let us love one another: for love is of God; and every one that loveth is born of God, and knoweth God.
     He that loveth not, knoweth not God; for God is love.

ST JOHN

APRIL 3   *Today is the birthdate of George Herbert, author of this hymn.*

> Teach me, my God and King,
> In all things thee to see;
> And what I do in anything
> To do it as for thee.

APRIL 4   It is told that the Baal Shem was once obliged to celebrate the Sabbath in the open fields. A herd of sheep were grazing not far off. When he spoke the blessing ... the sheep stood on their hind legs and remained in this position, turning towards the Master, until he had ended his prayer. For during the time while each creature was listening, it was in the primeval attitude in which it stands at the throne of God.

This story about the great Hasidic rabbi, the Baal Shem, told by Martin Buber, resembles tales of St Francis of Assisi. Saints and mystics of many religions recognize that God is not just for our own species. We share Him with other animals and with creation.

APRIL

This is the sum of things – that we
A lifetime live greatheartedly,
See the whole best that life has meant
Do out our work, and go content.

ARTHUR W. JOSE

APRIL 5

However mean your life is, meet it and live it; do not shun it and call it hard names. It looks poorest when you are richest. Love your life, poor as it is. You may perhaps have some pleasant, thrilling, glorious hours, even in a poorhouse. The setting sun is reflected from the windows of the almshouse as brightly as from the rich man's abode. I do not see but a quiet mind may live as contentedly there, and have as cheering thoughts, as in a palace.

HENRY DAVID THOREAU

APRIL 6

Yet here is peace for ever new!
When I who watch them am away,
Still all things in this glade go through
The changes of their quiet day.

Then to their happy rest they pass;
The flowers upclose, the birds are fed,
The night comes down upon the grass,
The child sleeps warmly in his bed.

APRIL 7

Matthew Arnold wrote this in Kensington Gardens, watching birds and children, finding an oasis of serenity in the middle of London.

APRIL 8

O Lord,
Thou has given me a body,
Wherein the glory of Thy power shineth,
Wonderfully composed above the beasts,
Within distinguished into useful parts,
Beautified without with many ornaments.
Limbs rarely poised,
And made for heaven:
Veins wherein blood floweth
Refreshing all my flesh,
Like rivers.

Thomas Traherne called this poem 'Thanksgiving for the Body'. I can forget only too easily the wonder of my body and how it works.

APRIL 9

The three phrases I should never let into my mind, if I want to be happy, are: 'What if? If only? Why me?'

AUTHOR UNKNOWN

APRIL 10

A comely sight indeed it is to see
A world of blossoms on an apple tree.

JOHN BUNYAN

APRIL 11

There is not so poor a creature, but may be thy glass to see God in. If every gnat that flies were an archangel, all that could but tell me that there is a God; and the poorest worm that creeps tells me that.

JOHN DONNE

What is the use of April — what the use
Of her wild dreams, unless you bear your part?
The spring has let a thousand voices loose,
And shall not one find way into your heart.

GERALD GOULD

If we want a example we can find it at our own fireside. The love, the forgivingness, the loyalty and the cheerfulness of a dog, says the poet Robert Burns, is such that few of us can match him.

Man is the god of the dog. He knows no other; he can understand no other. And see how he worships him — with what reverence he crouches at his feet, with what love he fawns upon him, with what dependence he looks up to him, with what cheerful alacrity he obeys him. His whole soul is wrapt up in his god. Divines tells us that it just ought to be so with the Christian, but the dog puts the Christian to shame.

APRIL 14 *A small verse by Christina Rossetti describes so well the way we can, if we choose, notice the miracle of very ordinary sights.*

> Where innocent bright-eyes daisies are,
> With blades of grass between,
> Each daisy stands up like a star
> Out of a sky of green.

APRIL 15 I have three treasures;
Guard them and keep them safe:
    The first is Love.
    The second is, Never too much.
    The third is, Never be the first in the world.
Through love, one has no fear.
Through not doing too much, one has amplitude (of
    reserve power);
Through not presuming to be first in the world,
One can develop one's talent and let it mature.

LAO TSE

If your nose is close to the grindstone
And you hold it there long enough,
In time you'll say there's no such thing
As brooks that babble and birds that sing.
These three will all your world compose –
Just you, the stone and your poor old nose.

This piece of folk wisdom is popular because of its shrewd message. I am not living fully when I blot out reality with work.

If you want in your prayers to grouse, then for Christ's sake grouse. If you hate God, then for Christ's sake tell Him you do and tell Him why. By having the courage of your aggression you will show greater trust in Him and greater love for him than by all that 'resigned submissive meek' stuff which leaves you to take the hell out of other people, and not least out of yourself.

Though this advice from Harry A. Williams is Christian, I think it's useful for all who want to have more trust in their God.

Let my voice ring out and over the earth,
Through all the grief and strife,
With a golden joy in a silver mirth:
Thank God for Life.

JAMES THOMSON

The poorest way to face life is to face it with a sneer.

THEODORE ROOSEVELT

APRIL 20 *Thirteen-year-old Alice Ruddock sewed this verse on her sampler in 1736. The embroidery is in a Cambridge museum.*

> Life is happy; hear the birds.
> Early as the morning breaks,
> Every sweet-toned throat of silver
> Into songs of gladness breaks.

APRIL 21 Why destroy present happiness by a distant misery, which may never come at all, or you may never live to see it? For every substantial grief has twenty shadows and most of them shadows of your own making.

SYDNEY SMITH

APRIL 22 Rather stand up, assured with conscious pride,
Alone, than err with millions on thy side.

I have always felt ashamed when others disapprove of me, even if I am right. This couplet by the eighteenth-century poet Charles Churchill helps me to have the courage to face disapproval.

APRIL 23 What delights, what emancipates, not what scares and pains us, is wise and good in speech and in the arts. For, truly, the heart at the centre of the universe with every throb hurls the flood of happiness into every artery, vein, and veinlet, so that the whole system is inundated with the tides of joy.

Ralph Waldo Emerson says we should trust our own delight. If the way I am living makes me happy and free, it must be right.

The chief secret of comfort lies in not suffering trifles to vex us; and in prudently cultivating an undergrowth of small pleasures.

RICHARD SHARP

The poet Christopher Smart wrote blank verse of strange beauty. *When I read these lines, my heart feels the truths they express even when I am not sure of the words' literal meaning.*

For the flowers are great blessings ...
For the flowers have their angels even the words of God's
   creation.
For the warp and woof of flowers are worked by
   perpetual moving spirits.
For flowers are good both for the living
   and the dead.
For there is a language of flowers.
For there is a sound reasoning
   upon all flowers.
For elegant phrases are nothing
   but flowers.
For flowers are peculiarly the
   poetry of Christ.
For flowers are medicinal.
For flowers are musical in
   ocular harmony.

<u>APRIL 26</u> It will be a marvellous thing – the true personality of man. It will grow naturally and simply, flower-like, or as a tree grows. It will not be at discord. It will never argue or dispute. It will not prove things. It will know everything. And yet it will not busy itself about knowledge. Its value will not be measured by material things. The personality of man will be very wonderful. It will be as wonderful as the personality of a child.

OSCAR WILDE

<u>APRIL 27</u>

Be kind to each other!
The night's coming on,
When friend and when brother
Perchance may be gone!

Let falsehood assail not,
Nor envy disprove –
Let trifles prevail not
Against those ye love.

CHARLES SWAIN

Always be interested in whatever you undertake or may be doing for the moment. Dismiss from your mind everything else but the one thing you are doing at the time, and think only of that thing in all its bearings, and master it.

This is good advice from Thomas Edison. Single-minded concentration on the task at hand brings happiness with it.

Fall, showers of sweet delight;
Spring, flowers of pleasant mirth;
What heaven hath beams that shine more bright?
Here heaven is now, stars shine on earth.

THOMAS CAMPION

One of the most mysterious stories in the Old Testament concerns the prophet Elijah, waiting on Mount Horeb. God speaks to him, and sometimes to us today, in a small voice. Let us not ignore it.

And, behold, the Lord passed by, and a great and strong wind rent the mountains, and brake in pieces the rocks before the Lord; but the Lord was not in the wind: and after the wind, an earthquake; but the Lord was not in the earthquake;

And after the earthquake a fire; but the Lord was not in the fire: and after the fire a still small voice.

And it was so, when Elijah heard it, that he wrapped his face in his mantle, and went out, and stood in the entering in of the cave. And, behold, there came a voice unto him, and said, 'What doest thou here, Elijah?'

MAY

MAY 1

Life with yon lambs, like day, is just begun,
Yet nature seems to them a heavenly guide.
Does joy approach? They meet the coming tide;
And sullenness avoid, as now they shun
Pale twilight's lingering glooms, – and in the sun
Couch near their dams, with quiet satisfied;
Or gamble – each with his shadow at his side,
Varying its shape wherever he may run.
As they from turf yet hoar with sleepy dew
All turn, and court the shining and the green,
Where herbs look up, and opening flowers are seen;
Why to God's goodness cannot we be true,
And so, His gifts and promises between,
Feed to the last on pleasures ever new?

This sonnet was written by William Wordsworth on a May morning in 1838. He had been watching the lambs and wondering why we humans cannot live as simply and as joyfully as they do.

MAY 2

There are two ways of being happy. We may either diminish our wants or augment our means – either will do – the result is the same. If you are wise you will do both at the same time; and if you are very wise you will do both in such a way as to augment the general happiness of society.

BENJAMIN FRANKLIN

MAY 3   *This odd poem by John Hall pleases me because I love the idea of snails and fish, not just birds, paying tribute to the glory of God.*

> Happy choristers of air,
> Who by your nimble flight draw near
> His throne, Whose wondrous story,
> And unconfinèd glory
> Your notes still carol, Whom your sound
> And Whom your plumy pipes rebound.
>
> Yet do the lazy snails no less
> The greatness of our Lord confess.
> And those whom weight hath chained,
> And to the earth restrained,
> Their ruder voices do as well,
> Yea, and the speechless fishes tell.

MAY 4   Go with events, rather than struggle against them. Work with your virtues, rather than against your faults.

ANONYMOUS

MAY 5

I am content, I do not care,
Wag as it will the world for me;
When fuss and fret was all my fare,
It got no ground, as I could see.
So when away my caring went,
I counted cost and was content.

This pithy verse by John Byrom reminds me not to fuss and fret, which achieves nothing, merely making me unhappy, angry and upset.

MAY 6

We may not go to heaven in feather beds; it is not the way.

SIR THOMAS MORE

MAY 7

True kindness is a pure divine affinity,
Not founded upon human consanguinity.
It is a spirit, not a blood relation,
Superior to family and station.

HENRY DAVID THOREAU

MAY 8

Alexander Elchaninov was a remarkable Russian orthodox priest who had the gift of throwing a new light on common situations.

What must we do in order not to be bored with people? We must understand that God accomplishes His will concerning us through the persons whom He sends us. There are no accidental meetings; either God sends us a person we need or we are sent to someone by God, without our being aware of it.

MAY 9

Truth is within ourselves; it takes no rise
From outward things, whate'er you may believe.
There is an inmost centre in us all,
Where truth abides in fullness.

ROBERT BROWNING

MAY 10

God is always present and waiting to be discovered now, in the present moment, precisely where we are and in what we are doing.

HARRY A. WILLIAMS

MAY 11

These lines by Hartley Coleridge, son of the poet, remind me that unless I free the inner child in myself, I will not enjoy life fully.

O what a wilderness were this sad world
If man were ever man, and never child.

MAY 12

A man should himself realize that conflict-situations between himself and others are nothing but the effects of conflict-situations in his own soul; then he should try to overcome this inner conflict, so that afterwards he may go out to his fellow men and enter into new, transformed relationships with them. The essential thing is to begin with oneself.

If our relationships are to be happier, the effort must begin with ourselves, as Martin Buber points out. We must have the courage to be the first, perhaps the only one, to change. We cannot make others different; we can change our own attitudes and behaviour.

It is a mistake to suppose that men succeed through success; <u>MAY 13</u>
they much oftener succeed through failure.

*I find it so difficult to remember this truth, pointed out here by Samuel
Smiles. Our mistakes teach us much more than successes.*

I come in the little things, <u>MAY 14</u>
Saith the Lord:
Yea! on the glancing wings
Of eager birds, the softly pattering feet
Of furred and gentle beasts, I come to meet
Your hard and wayward heart. In bright brown eyes
That peep from out the brake, I stand confest.
On every nest
Where feathery Patience is content to brood
And leaves her pleasure for the high emprize
Of motherhood —
There doth My Godhead rest.

EVELYN UNDERHILL

MAY 15   *In the writings of Imam Hazrat Ali, the fourth Caliph of Islam and the son-in-law of the Prophet Muhammad, the bee is an example of cleanliness and lightness of touch. In the West the bee has often been seen as hard-working. Yet how important is a light touch.*

Be like the bee; anything he eats is clean, anything he drops is sweet, and any branch he sits on does not break.

MAY 16   At the close of life the question is –
Not how much you have got,
But how much you have given.
Not how much you have won,
But how much you have done.
Not how much you have saved,
But how much you have sacrificed.
Not how much you were honoured,
But how much you have loved and served.

AUTHOR UNKNOWN

The chief obstacle to the enjoyment of life is its dullness and the weariness which invades us because there is nothing to be seen or done of any particular value. If the supernatural becomes natural and the natural becomes supernatural, the world regains its splendour and charm.

MARK RUTHERFORD

If Nature put not forth her power
About the opening of the flower,
Who is it that could live an hour?

ALFRED, LORD TENNYSON

If men should lay all their evils together, to be afterwards by equal portions divided among them, most men would rather take that they brought there, than stand to the division.

I take these words seriously since they were written by Robert Southwell, a martyr for his faith, while he was in prison.

John Greenleaf Whittier wrote this verse for a sundial belonging to a friend. Sometimes it is through our pain (the shadow, not the light in our lives) that we can feel God working in our being.

With warning hand I mark time's rapid flight
From life's glad morning to its solemn night;
Yet, through the dear God's love, I also show
There's light above me by the shade below.

MAY 21 Selfishness is not living as one wishes to live; it is asking others to live as one wishes to live. And unselfishness is letting other people's lives alone, not interfering with them.

Wisdom from Oscar Wilde. At times this is difficult to remember.

MAY 22
Retired from crowded courts, is it not sweet
To find the daisy scattered at thy feet?

These two lines by John Joseph Briggs remind me of one of May's common pleasures. Let me not walk through life blind to daisies.

MAY 23 *One of the earliest and most talented American poets was Anne Bradstreet. As well as writing verse, she made a collection of pithy sayings and short pieces of wisdom. This is one of them.*

A shadow in the parching sun and a shelter in a blustering storm are of all seasons the most welcome; so a faithful friend in time of adversity is of all other most comfortable.

MAY 24
Let praise devote thy work, and skill employ
Thy whole mind, and thy heart be lost in joy ...
Man doeth nothing well, be it great or small,
Save to praise God; but that hath savèd all.
For God requires no more than thou hast done,
And takes thy work to bless it for his own.

There is a way of working wholeheartedly, says Robert Bridges, which transforms any task or occupation into a true delight.

Forgiveness is another word for letting go. We are saved by forgiveness, the power to forgive ourselves, to allow ourselves to be forgiven, which matures into the power to forgive others and allow them their time to be forgiven. Forgiveness is about letting go of guilt – some imagined, some real – and about letting go of fear. There is no healing, no salvation, without forgiveness. And with forgiveness all things become saved and healed once again. Creation is restored.

MATTHEW FOX

It is so difficult to achieve inner serenity. Sometimes the news on *television or in newspapers disturbs us. There is a glimpse of possible serenity in Mary Coleridge's poem, 'No Newspapers'.*

Where, to me, is the loss
Of the scenes they saw –
   of the sounds they
   heard;
A butterfly flits across
Or a bird.
The moss is growing on the
   wall,
I heard the leaf of a poppy fall.

MAY 27   I celebrate myself, and sing myself,
And what I assume you shall assume,
For every atom belonging to me as good belongs to you.

I loafe and invite my soul,
I lean and loafe at my ease observing a spear of summer
grass.
My tongue, every atom of my blood, formed from this soil,
this air,
Born here of parents born here from parents the same, and
their parents the same,
I, now thirty-seven years old in perfect health begin,
Hoping to cease not till death.

Today I too will celebrate myself like the poet, Walt Whitman.

MAY 28   Prayer enlarges the heart until it is capable of containing God's
gift of Himself. Ask and seek, and your heart will grow big
enough to receive Him and keep Him as your own.

MOTHER TERESA OF CALCUTTA

Just as religious believers can be spiritually comatose, so atheists and   MAY 29
agnostics can have living spiritual resources. A life without a God need
not be a life without meaning. This remark by Albert Einstein describes
a spiritual attitude possible to anybody.

It is enough for me to contemplate the mystery of conscious life perpetuating itself through all eternity; to reflect upon the marvellous structure of the universe, which we can dimly perceive, and to try humbly to comprehend even an infinitesimal part of the intelligence manifested in nature.

We need not always be out of doors to enjoy beauty. Walter de la   MAY 30
Mare wrote a lovely poem about the beauty of a flower in a vase.

> A rose, in water, to its stem
> Decoys a myriad beads of air;
> And, lovely with the light on them,
> Gives even its thorns their share.

Verily I say unto you, except ye turn, and become as little   MAY 31
children, ye shall in no wise enter into the kingdom of heaven.
    Whosoever therefore shall humble himself as this little child, the same is greatest in the kingdom of heaven.
    And whoso shall receive one such little child in my name, receiveth me ...
    See that ye despise not one of these little ones.

Jesus of Nazareth said this, when he was asked who was the greatest in
the kingdom of heaven. These words are from the revised version of the
Bible, where I think they are clearest.

JUNE

In June 'tis good to lie beneath a tree
While the blithe season comforts every sense,
Steeps all the brain in rest, and heals the heart,
Brimming it o'er with sweetness unawares.

JUNE 1

In the fret and bustle of ordinary life, I often forget to pause for a while, take a break, and heal my heart, as James Russell Lowell suggests. It is healing just to sit on the grass or under a tree.

There is something called the 'As if' principle, which helps us to change our lives. Here Norman Vincent Peale explains how the 'As if' principle can change first behaviour then inward attitudes.

JUNE 2

This means simply that by acting as you wish yourself to be, in due course you will become as you act. If you are fearful, act as if you had courage. Continue to act courageously and ultimately your fear will diminish as courage increases. If you are inclined to criticize, start acting generously, placing the best connotation on everyone and everything, and you will become less critical and more compassionate. The principle operates similarly in the matter of increasing enthusiasm. Begin to act enthusiastically. At first the effort may appear ineffective and even phony or insincere, inasmuch as you do not feel enthusiastic. But persevere and surprisingly, you will become increasingly enthusiastic.

<u>JUNE 3</u> *In 1854 Chief Seattle, leader of various native American tribes in Washington State, wrote a letter to the President who was negotiating to buy his land. This is part of it. A century later we still need the courage to acknowledge and act on what he wrote.*

How can you buy or sell the sky, the warmth of the land?
    The idea is strange to us.
If we do not own the freshness of the air and the sparkle
    of the water, how can you buy them?
Every part of this earth is sacred to my people.
We are part of the earth and it is part of us. The
    perfumed flowers are our sisters; the deer, the horse, the
    great eagle, these are our brothers.
Whatever befalls the earth befalls the sons of the earth. If
    men spit upon the ground, they spit upon themselves.
All things are connected like the blood which unites one
    family. All things are connected.

<u>JUNE 4</u>

It is as healthy to enjoy sentiment as to enjoy jam.

G.K. CHESTERTON

O may I with myself agree,
And never covet what I see:
Content me with an humble shade,
My passions tamed, my wishes laid;
For while our wishes wildly roll,
We banish quiet from the soul.

JOHN DYER

Another exercise is to sit, concentrating all your attention on the physical feelings of breathing in and breathing out, without deliberately changing the rhythm of your breathing. Focus attention on feeling the cold air entering your nostrils and the warm air when you exhale ... In itself it is a very good relaxation exercise, but if you care to use it for more explicit prayer, then let the in-breathing express all that you long for in life, however impossible it may seem in practice, and let the out-breath express your surrender of everything to God, all of your life with its worries, sins, guilt and regrets. Again, it is very important to do this without self-judgement, whether of approval or disapproval. Keep your attention fixed on your desire to hand over all these worries about self.

GERARD W. HUGHES

Live and learn,
Not first learn and then live, is our concern.

ROBERT BROWNING

JUNE 8   *Locked up in an asylum after he had gone mad, the poet John Clare wrote this fragment of verse about the beauties of nature.*

> Her flowers …
> They are her very Scriptures upon earth,
> And teach us simple mirth where'er we go;
> Even in prison they can solace me,
> For where they bloom God is, and I am free.

JUNE 9   Be strong and of a good courage; be not afraid, neither be thou dismayed; for the Lord thy God is with thee whithersoever thou goest.

JOSHUA

JUNE 10
> There are thousands to tell you it cannot be done,
> There are thousands to prophesy failure;
> There are thousands to point out to you, one by one,
> The dangers that wait to assail you.
> But just buckle right in with a bit of a grin,
> Then take off your coat and go to it.
> Just start in to sing, as you tackle the thing
> That cannot be done, and you'll do it.

ANONYMOUS

JUNE 11   The secret of my success is that at an early age I discovered I was not God.

This remark by the American essayist Oliver Wendell Holmes is comic, but it also has something serious to say. Think about it.

JUNE

JUNE 12

The wisdom of the Hasidic rabbis appeals to me. Here is something said by the maggid (that is the preacher) of Zlotchov in Galicia.

Just as our fathers founded new ways of serving, each a new service according to his character; one the service of love, the other that of stern justice, the third that of beauty, so each one of us in his own way shall devise something new in the light of teachings and of service, and do what has not yet been done.

JUNE 13

He came and took me by the hand
Up to the red rose tree,
He kept His meaning to Himself
But gave a rose to me.
I did not pray Him to lay bare
The mystery to me,
Enough the rose was heaven to smell
And His own face to see.

RALPH HODGSON

JUNE 14

Yet seek Him, in His favour life is found;
All bliss beside, a shadow or a sound:
Then heaven, eclipsed so long, and this dull earth
Shall seem to start into a second birth;
Nature, assuming a more lovely face,
Borrowing a beauty from the works of grace,
Shall be despised and overlooked no more,
Shall fill thee with delights unfelt before,
Impart to things inanimate a voice,
And bid her mountains and her hills rejoice;
The sound shall run along the winding vales,
And thou enjoy an Eden, ere it fails.

WILLIAM COWPER

JUNE 15   Life appears to me to be too short to be spent in nursing
animosity or in registering wrongs.

CHARLOTTE BRONTË

When you compare yourself with others, the comparison is almost always to your own disadvantage. For you are comparing your inside (for instance, how you feel inside) with their outside (the brave face they are putting on their own fear).

AUTHOR UNKNOWN

The man who because of his own wisdom looks down on
others has never won men's hearts.
The man who in spite of his own wisdom is humble to
others has never failed to win men's hearts.

Another ancient saying from Lao Tse, the Taoist philosopher who lived three centuries before the birth of Jesus Christ.

All that is in heaven is also on earth.

For me there is a wealth of meaning in this sentence by the philosopher Plotinus. I can look for heavenly things here and now.

I love to mark the floweret's eye,
To rest where pebbles form my bed,
Where shapes and colours scattered lie
In varying millions round my head.
The soul rejoices when alone,
And feels her glorious empire free;
Sees God in every shining stone
And revels in variety.

ROBERT BLOOMFIELD

JUNE 20   The first and worst of all frauds is to cheat
One's self.

Philip James Bailey points out the cost of inner denial. We harm ourselves each time we are less than truly honest with ourselves.

JUNE 21   Oh what an humble garb true joy puts on! Those who want happiness must stoop to find it; it is a flower that grows in every vale.

WILLIAM BLAKE

JUNE 22   *This anonymous verse was written in the fly leaf of a Bible.*

Could we with ink the ocean fill,
Were every stalk on earth a quill,
And were the skies of parchment made,
And every man a scribe by trade,
To tell the love of God alone
Would drain the ocean dry.
Nor could a scroll contain the whole
Though stretched from sky to sky.

JUNE 23   *Before his death at the stake, Thomas Cranmer said this:*

I pray you, learn and bear well away this one lesson, to do good unto all men, as much as in you lieth, and to hurt no man, no more than you would hurt your own natural loving brother or sister ... Whosoever hateth any person, and goeth about maliciously to hinder or hurt him, surely, God is not with that man.

Yes, light is lovely for its own good sake.
Morning is morning still, clouded or fair.

LEIGH HUNT

Gather a single blade of grass, and examine for a minute, quietly, its narrow sword-shaped strip of fluted green. Nothing, as it seems there, of notable goodness or beauty. A very little strength, and a very little tallness, and a few delicate long lines meeting in a point. And yet, think of it well, and judge whether of all the gorgeous flowers that beam in summer air, and of all strong and goodly trees, pleasant to the eyes or good for food, there be any by man so deeply loved, by God so highly graced as this narrow point of feeble green. Consider what we owe merely to the meadow grass, to the covering of the dark ground by that glorious enamel, by the companies of these soft, and countless, and peaceful spears.

JOHN RUSKIN

JUNE 26   *Some people find Gerard Manley Hopkins difficult but read him without anxiety and the meaning will come. This is a hymn of praise.*

> Glory be to God for dappled things —
> For skies of couple-colour as a brindled cow;
> For rose-moles all in stipple upon trout that swim;
> Fresh-firecoal chestnut-falls; finches' wings;
> Landscape plotted and pieced — fold, fallow, and plough;
> And áll trádes, their gear and tackle and trim.
> All things counter, original, spare, strange;
> Whatever is fickle, freckled (who knows how?)
> With swift, slow; sweet, sour; adazzle, dim;
> He fathers-forth whose beauty is past change:
>   Praise him.

JUNE 27   Great works are performed not by strength but by perseverance.

SAMUEL JOHNSON

If you hold on to anything too tightly, you become its prisoner. JUNE 28

AUTHOR UNKNOWN

Old things need not be therefore true, JUNE 29
O brother men, nor yet the new:
Ah, still awhile the thought retain,
And yet consider it again.

The souls of now two thousand years
Have laid up here their toils and fears,
And all the earnings of their pain:
Ah, yet consider it again.

We! What do we see? Each a space
Of some few yards before his face;
Does that the whole wide plan explain?
Ah, yet consider it again.

Arthur Hugh Clough argues against hiding in old habits of thought or grabbing at the new. There's a saying — Think, think, think.

Is it not easy to conceive the world in your mind? To think the JUNE 30
heavens fair? The sun glorious? The earth fruitful? The air
pleasant? And the Giver bountiful? Yet these are the things
which it is difficult to retain. For would we always be sensible
of their use and value; we should be always delighted with the
wealth and glory.

THOMAS TRAHERNE

JULY

And summer came, and every weed
Of great or little had its meed;
Without its leaves there wa'n't a bower
Nor one poor weed without its flower.
'Twas love and pleasure all along;
I felt that I'd a right to song ...
For everything I felt a love,
The weeds below, the birds above;
The weeds that bloomed in summer's hours
I thought they should be reckoned flowers;
They made a garden free for all
And so I loved them great and small.

John Clare describes a spiritual attitude, when the smallest weed is charged with glory. This calms my anxiety and builds serenity.

The old tales of the saints often include stories of how their tenderness included all beings. Here is St George of Suelli.

The loving kindness and pity possessed by this holy man was extended not only to men but to the birds which fly in the air. Sparrows, parched with thirst, used to pant in this dry place without any hope of cooling their tongues; for that spot is utterly devoid of water. So he struck a rock with his staff and such an abundant spring flowed out that it neither increased with rain, nor was diminished by the burning rays of the sun.

In heavenly love abiding,
No change my heart shall fear;
And safe is such confiding,
For nothing changes here:
The storm may roar without me,
My heart may low be laid;
But God is round about me,
And can I be dismayed?

Wherever He may guide me,
No want shall turn me back;
My Shepherd is
beside me,
And nothing can I
lack:
His wisdom ever
waketh,
His sight is never
dim;
He knows the way
He taketh,
And I will walk
with him.

A lovely hymn by Anna Laetitia Waring based on the Psalm 23.

The laughter of man is the contentment of God.

John Weiss reminds us that God wants us to be happy and joyful.

The greatest of faults, I should say, is to be conscious of none.   JULY 5

When I am cast down by my shortcomings, I find this saying by Thomas Carlyle comforting.

Not in the solitude   JULY 6
Alone, may man commune with heaven, or see
Only in savage wood
And sunny vale the present Deity;
Or only hear his voice
Where the winds whisper and the waves rejoice.

Even here do I behold
Thy steps, Almighty — here amidst the crowd
Through the great city rolled,
With everlasting murmur deep and loud.

WILLIAM CULLEN BRYANT

O God, help us not to despise or oppose what we do not   JULY 7
understand.

WILLIAM PENN

One thing at a time   JULY 8
And that done well,
Is a very good rule
As many can tell.

ANONYMOUS

JULY 9

'Live while you live,' the Epicure would say,
'And seize the pleasures of the present day.'
'Live while you live,' the sacred preacher cries,
'And give to God each moment as it flies.'
Lord, in my views let both united be;
I live in pleasure, when I live to Thee.

PHILIP DODDRIDGE

JULY 10

The foundation of content must spring up in a man's own mind; and he who has so little knowledge of human nature as to seek happiness by changing everything but his own disposition, will waste his life in fruitless effort, and multiply the griefs which he purposes to remove.

SAMUEL JOHNSON

JULY 11

Don't forget
That the cowslip, rose and violet
Are Facts of Life, as well ...

RALPH HODGSON

JULY 12

That a thing is true is no reason that it should be said, but that it should be done; that it should be acted upon; that it should be made our own inwardly.

This comes from the Parochial and Plain Sermons of Cardinal John Henry Newman. I must make every effort not to be a talker but a doer. Best show my ideals by my behaviour not my words.

JULY

Let me be just and true in all my dealings. Let no mean or low thought have a moment's place in my mind. Let my word be my bond. Let me take no unchivalrous advantage of anyone. Let me be generous in my judgement. Let me be loyal and courageous.

This anonymous passage comes from a commonplace book kept by Mrs Evelyn Thomas, who generously shared it with me.

The moon and the stars,
Dew and rain,
Hills and alleys,
Fields and meadows,
In serving fishes, fowls and
    beasts,
Serve all the sons of Men
A new deep and richer way.
And in serving them, bless,
    enrich, serve me, Thy
    servant.

This is part of 'The Thanksgivings', a mystic prose poem by Thomas Traherne, a clergyman of the seventeenth century.

JULY 15

Here's an example from
A butterfly;
That on a rough, hard rock
Happy can lie;
Friendless and all alone
On this unsweetened stone.

Now let my bed be hard,
No care take I;
I'll make my joy like this
Small butterfly;
Whose happy heart has power
To make a stone a flower.

W.H. DAVIES

JULY 16   There is something that can only be found in one place. It is a
great treasure, which may be called the fulfilment of existence.
The place where this treasure can be found is the place on
which one stands.

MARTIN BUBER

If I am weak, yet God is strong,
If I am false, yet God is true.
Old things are past, or right or wrong,
And every day that comes is new.
Tomorrow then fresh hope may bring,
And rise with healing on its wing.

Hartley Coleridge, who wrote this verse, was the son of the poet Samuel Coleridge. He struggled with alcoholism all his life.

When we wish to know if a man may be accounted happy we should perhaps inquire, not whether he is prosperous or unprosperous, but how much he is affected by little things – by such as hourly assail us in the commerce of life, and are no more to be regarded than the buzzings and stingings of a summer fly.

SAMUEL ROGERS

Love can tell, and love alone,
Whence the million stars were strewn,
Why each atom knows its own,
How, in spite of woe and death,
Gay is life, and sweet is breath.

ROBERT BRIDGES

Haste not, be at rest, this Now is eternity.

Richard Jefferies, the nature writer and novelist, found his vision of eternity in the beauty of nature and in his own self.

JULY 21

I believe in the flesh and the appetites.
Seeing, hearing, feeling, are miracles, and each
part and tag of me is a miracle.

WALT WHITMAN

JULY 22

True life is lived when changes occur.

I like this thought from Leo Tolstoy. Perhaps both outer and inner changes, even painful ones, make me more fully alive.

JULY 23

Serene will be our days and bright,
And happy will our nature be,
When love is an unerring light,
And joy its own security.
And they a blissful course may hold
Even now, who, not unwisely bold,
Live in the spirit of this creed;
Yet seek thy firm support, according to
their need.

WILLIAM WORDSWORTH

JULY 24

I do the very best I know how – the very best I can – and I mean to keep doing so until the end. If the end brings me out all right, what is said against me won't amount to anything; if the end brings me out wrong, ten angels swearing I was right would make no difference.

How easy it is to worry what others think. Yet if we are to follow the path that is right for us, there will be times when, like Abraham Lincoln, we must press on despite the misunderstanding of others.

Those who are enlightened with the true light are not so anxious and eager to accomplish much and with all speed, but rather seek to do things in peace and good leisure; and if some not weighty matter be neglected, they do not therefore think themselves lost, for they know very well that order and fitness are better than disorder, and therefore they choose to walk orderly, yet know at the same time that their salvation hangeth not thereon. Therefore they are not in so great anxiety.

From Theologica Germanica, *an anonymous medieval treatise. Let me live serenely, avoiding both disorder and obsessive order.*

Gentle nature seems to love us
In each fair and finished scene,
All is beauteous blue above us,
All beneath is cheerful green.

A verse from the hymns and spiritual songs of Christopher Smart. The childlike simplicity of his perception moves me.

JULY 27

I see His blood upon the rose
And in the stars the glory of His eyes,
His body gleams amid eternal snows,
His tears fall from the skies.

I see His face in every flower;
The thunder and the singing of the birds
Are but His voice — and carven by His power
Rocks are His written words.

All pathways by His feet are worn,
His strong heart stirs the ever-beating sea,
His crown of thorns is twined with every thorn,
His cross is every tree.

JOSEPH PLUNKETT

JULY 28 The tragedy of life is not so much what men suffer, but rather
what they miss.

THOMAS CARLYLE

And the Lord, He it is that doth go before thee; He will be
with thee, and He will not fail thee, neither forsake thee: fear
not, neither be dismayed.

DEUTERONOMY

Flowers seem intended for the solace of ordinary humanity:
children love them; quiet, tender, contented ordinary people love
them as they grow; luxurious and disorderly people rejoice in
them gathered. They are the cottager's treasure; and in the
crowded town, mark the windows of the workers in whose
heart rests the covenant of peace.

JOHN RUSKIN

Riches we wish to get,
Yet remain spendthrifts still;
We would have health, and yet
Still use our bodies ill;
Bafflers of our own prayers, from
    youth to life's last scenes.

We would have inward peace,
Yet will not look within;
We would have misery cease,
Yet will not cease from sin;
We want all pleasant ends, but will
    use no harsh means;

We want the results of change, but are not willing to work for it, says
Matthew Arnold. Give me the courage to look within.

AUGUST

I hope, friend, you and I are not too proud to ask for our daily bread, and to be grateful for getting it? Mr Philip had to work for his, in care and trouble, like other children of men: – to work for it, and I hope to pray for it too. It is a thought to me awful and beautiful, that of the daily prayer, and of the myriads of fellow men uttering it, in care and in sickness, in doubt and in poverty, in health and in wealth. All over this world what an endless chorus is singing of love, and thanks, and prayer. As thy sun rises, friend, over the humble housetops round about your home, shall you wake many and many a day to duty and labour. May the task have been honestly done when the night comes.

Today is Lammas Day, traditionally marked by thanksgiving for bread and corn. The original name was Loafmass day. Here are William Thackeray's thoughts on 'Give us today our daily bread'.

The tiniest living thing
That soars on feathered wing,
Or crawls among the long grass out of sight
Has just as good a right
To its appointed portion of delight
As any King.

A lovely thought from Christina Rossetii. In the grass we sit on tiny insects are living out their little portion of delight.

AUGUST 3   *George Fox, the founder of the Quaker movement, went through a time of spiritual suffering in which he was painfully conscious of evil. Yet from this he found a new trust in and openness to God.*

I saw also that there was an ocean of darkness and death, but an infinite ocean of light and love which flowed over the ocean of darkness. In that also I saw the infinite love of God; and I had great openings.

AUGUST 4   *When I see the butterflies visiting the garden flowers in late summer I remember Samuel Rogers' poem to a butterfly.*

Child of the sun! pursue thy rapturous flight,
Mingling with her thou lov'st in fields of light;
And, where the flowers of paradise unfold,
Quaff fragrant nectar from their cups of gold.
There shall thy wings, rich as an evening sky,
Expand and shut with silent ecstasy!
– Yet wert thou once a worm, a thing that crept
On the bare earth, then wrought a tomb and slept.
And such is man; soon from his cell of clay
To burst a seraph in the blaze of day.

AUGUST

Our sages say: 'Seek peace in your own place.' You cannot find peace anywhere save in your own self. In the psalm we read: 'There is no peace in my bones because of my sin.' When a man has made peace within himself, he will be able to make peace in the whole world.

AUGUST 5

RABBI BUNAM

To love and to be loved the wise would give
All that for which alone the unwise live.

AUGUST 6

WALTER SAVAGE LANDOR

Cultivate simplicity, or rather, I should say, banish elaborateness; for simplicity springs spontaneous from the heart, and carries into daylight its own buds of genuine, sweet, and clear flowers of expression.

AUGUST 7

This was the advice Charles Lamb gave to his friend, the poet Samuel Coleridge. Simplicity improves not only the way we express ourselves but also our understanding of the world.

Snap, chord of manhood's tenser strain!
Today I will be a boy again;
The mind's pursuing element,
Like a bow slackened and unbent.

AUGUST 8

These lines by James Russell Lowell remind me that for a time I can choose to see and enjoy life as a child does, shaking off adult preoccupations. Taking an inner holiday like this refreshes me.

AUGUST 9

Rich music breathes in summer's every sound;
And in her harmony of varied greens,
Woods, meadows, hedgerows, cornfields, all around
Much beauty intervenes,
Filling with harmony the ear and eye,
While o'er the mingling scenes
Far spreads the laughing sky.

A verse by John Clare on the miracle of the natural world.

AUGUST 10

What matters in learning is not to be taught, but to wake up.

AUTHOR UNKNOWN

AUGUST 11

Set not the faults of other folks in view
But rather mind what thou thyself shouldst do;
For, twenty errors of thy neighbour known
Will tend but little to reform thine own.

JOHN BYROM

AUGUST 12

I am sorry for the man or woman who has never been touched
by the spell of this mysterious sensorial life, with its irrationality,
if so you like to call it, but its vigilance and its supreme felicity.
The holidays of life are its most vitally significant portions,
because they are, or at least should be, covered with just this
kind of magically irresponsible spell.

WILLIAM JAMES

AUGUST

For me, whom love and no unloving need
Have taught the treasures found in daily things,
I count the morning bright, if I but hear
One bird's voice sparkle.

LEIGH HUNT

An old man walking the beach at dawn noticed a young man
ahead of him picking up starfish and flinging
them into the sea. Catching up with
the youth he asked what he was
doing. 'The starfish will die if
they are still on the beach
when the sun roasts them
with its mid-morning
heat,' came the answer.
'But the beach goes on
for miles, and there
are millions of
starfish,' countered
the old man. 'How
can your effort make
any difference?' The
young man looked at
the starfish in his hand
and then threw it to
safety in the waves. 'It
makes a difference to this
one,' he said.

AUTHOR UNKNOWN

AUGUST 15

Look on yonder earth:
The golden harvests spring; the unfailing sun
Sheds light and life; the fruits, the flowers, the trees,
Arise in due succession; all things speak
Peace, harmony, and love. The universe,
In nature's silent eloquence, declares
That all fulfil the works of love and joy.

PERCY BYSSHE SHELLEY

AUGUST 16

I love the safety of routine. Yet I must learn to be flexible, to change as life changes. Ralph Waldo Emerson perceived this.

In nature every moment is new; the past is always swallowed and forgotten; the coming only is sacred. Nothing is secure but life, transition, the energizing spirit. People wish to be settled; only as far as they are unsettled is there any hope for them. Life is a series of surprises. Nothing great was ever achieved without enthusiasm. The way of life is wonderful; it is by abandonment.

AUGUST

AUGUST 17

I sometimes feel that it is a mistake to make a mistake. Yet some of my errors have transformed my life for good. This is why I rather like these words by the philosopher Friedrich Nietzsche.

Life is no argument; error might be among the conditions of life.

AUGUST 18

Who seeks to please all men each way
And not himself offend,
He may begin his work today
But God knows when he'll end.

LORD HOLLAND

AUGUST 19

There is an incessant influx of novelty into the world and yet we tolerate incredible dullness.

HENRY DAVID THOREAU

AUGUST 20

I hear at morn and even,
At noon and midnight hour,
The choral harmonies of heaven
Earth's Babel tongues o'erpower.

Then, then I feel that He,
(Remembered or forgot,)
The Lord is never far from me,
Though I perceive Him not.

These verses by an eighteenth-century poet, James Montgomery, remind me that God stays always close to me, whether I feel Him or not.

AUGUST 21 In beholding how the true calmness of life is changed into hurry and that many, by eagerly pursuing outward treasure, are in great danger of withering as to the inward state of the mind: I often feel pure love begets longings in my heart for the promoting an humble, plain, temperate way of living; a life where no unnecessary cares nor expenses may encumber our minds, nor lessen our ability to do good.

JOHN WOOLMAN

AUGUST 22

How dull it is to pause, to make an end,
To rust unburnish'd, not to shine in use!

These lines by Alfred, Lord Tennyson are about not giving up. Age is no reason for sloth. We should live to wear out, not rust out.

AUGUST 23 Looking into the fluffy white heart of an oleander the other day, a kind of rapture at its uselessness came over me, at the divine heedlessness of anything but glory and beauty in the making of it.

MARY COLERIDGE

AUGUST 24 *In a book,* Bless All thy Creatures, Lord*, by Richard Newman I found this prayer. Its author is unknown. Its spirit is love.*

Dear Father, hear and bless
Thy beasts and singing birds,
And guard with tenderness
Small things that have no words.

When all within is dark,
and former friends misprise;
From them I turn to You,
and find love in Your eyes.

AUGUST 25

When all within is dark,
and I my soul despise;
From me I turn to You,
and find love in Your eyes.

When all Your face is dark,
and Your just angers rise,
From You I turn to You
and find love in Your eyes.

These verses by Israel Abrahams are based on Ibn Gabirol's words.

We all like to forgive, and we all love best not those who offend us least, nor those who have done most for us, but those who make it most easy for us to forgive them.

AUGUST 26

SAMUEL BUTLER

AUGUST 27 *We can find beauty in the strangest places. On derelict town wastelands, as well as country hedgerows, bloom the flowers of the common bramble, here praised by the poet Ebenezer Elliott.*

> Thy fruit full well the schoolboy knows,
> Wild bramble of the brake!
> So put thou forth thy small white rose,
> I love it for his sake.
> Though woodbines flaunt, and roses glow
> Through all the fragrant bowers,
> Thou need'st not be ashamed to show
> Thy satin-threaded flowers;
> For dull the eye, the heart is dull,
> That cannot feel how fair,
> Amid all beauty beautiful
> Thy tender blossoms are.

AUGUST 28 Men who do good things are so much more valuable than those who say wise ones.

SYDNEY SMITH

Cast thy burden upon the Lord, and he shall sustain thee.

This single line from Psalm 55 is easier to read than to practise. I find it difficult to trust God and relax my concerns into His care.

To do the magnanimous thing
And take oneself by surprise
If oneself is not in the habit of him,
Is precisely the finest of joys —

Not to do the magnanimous thing,
Notwithstanding it never be known,
Notwithstanding it cost us existence once,
Is rapture herself spurn—

The poems of Emily Dickinson seem simple yet have quite difficult ideas. She is saying that if we turn away from doing the magnanimous action, even for sensible reasons, we are turning our back on rapture. We should aim at a kind of loving recklessness — because it is so good for us, rather than others.

When I would beget content and increase confidence in the power and wisdom and providence of Almighty God, I will walk the meadows by some gliding stream, and there contemplate the lilies that take no care, and those very many other little living creatures that are not only created, but fed (man knows not how) by the goodness of the God of nature, and therefore trust in Him.

IZAAK WALTON

SEPTEMBER

A haze on the far horizon,
The infinite, tender sky,
The ripe, rich tint of the cornfields,
And the wild geese flying high,
And over upland and lowland
The charm of the golden rod:
Some of us call it autumn,
And others call it God.

This verse by William Herbert Carruth speaks to me because of its spirituality. Thanksgiving doesn't need a worked-out theology.

To have blessings and to prize them is to be in heaven; to have them, and not to prize them, is to be in hell, I would say, upon earth. To prize them and not to have them, is to be in hell, which is evident by the effects. To prize blessings while we have them is to enjoy them, and the effect thereof is contentation, pleasure, thanksgiving, happiness. To prize them when they are gone produceth envy, covetousness, repining, ingratitude, vexation, misery. But it was no great mistake to say, that to have blessings, and not to prize them, is to be in hell. For it maketh them ineffectual, as if they were absent. Yea, in some respect it is worse than to be in hell. It is more irrational.

THOMAS TRAHERNE

<u>SEPTEMBER 3</u> Upon a fair, clear night, the sky garnished with stars out of number shineth goodly, which, and ye take heed, ye may see them twinkle as it were a candle or a taper burning, and among them the moon with her full light goeth forth by little and little, gliding softly. Be not these pleasant things?

A TUDOR TEXTBOOK

<u>SEPTEMBER 4</u> *This poetic definition of friendship is by the Elizabethan poet Richard Barnfield. Friends are a loving mirror, reflecting back to us what we feel, listening and validating us to ourselves.*

He that is thy friend indeed,
He will help thee in thy need:
If thou sorrow, he will weep:
If thou wake, he cannot sleep:
Thus of every grief, in heart,
He, with thee, doth bear a part.
These are certain signs to know
Faithful friend from flattering foe.

Live unto the dignity of thy nature.

This simple sentence by Sir Thomas Browne intrigues me. When I cannot live up to it, something in me or my life needs changing.

Sometime aright, and sometime wrong I go:
Sometime my pace is speedy, sometime slow;
Sometime I stagger, and sometime I fall:
Sometime I sing, sometime for help I call.
Now, I have courage and do nothing fear,
Anon my spirits half dejected are.
I doubt, and hope, and doubt, and hope again;
And many a change of passions I sustain
In this my journey: so, that now and then,
I lost may seem perhaps to other men.
Yea, to myself awhile, when sins impure
Do my Redeemer's love from me obscure.
But whatsoe'er betide, I know full well
My Father (who above the clouds do dwell)
An eye upon his wand'ring child doth cast;
And He will fetch me to my home at last.
For, of God's love a witness want not I;
And whom He loves, He loves eternally.

These lines were written by George Wither, a seventeenth-century poet whose life contained many failures and much faith.

Time spent on reconnaisance is never wasted.

This old army saying saves me much heartache when I remember it, and so pause to think things through before rushing to act.

SEPTEMBER 8

The common problem, yours, mine, everyone's,
Is — not to fancy what were fair in life
Provided it could be, — but, finding first
What may be, then find how to make it fair
Up to our means: a very different thing!

It is not easy to put into action the truth in these lines by Robert Browning — making beauty in our life just out of what we have.

SEPTEMBER 9

To the end of the longest life you are still a beginner.

A sentence by Cardinal John Henry Newman. A good life is never achieved. When I feel I have it made, that's the time to watch out.

SEPTEMBER 10

We live in deeds, not years: in thoughts, not breaths;
In feelings, not in figures on a dial.
We should count time by heart-throbs.
He most lives
Who thinks most, feels the noblest, acts the best.
Life's but a means unto an end — that end,
Beginning, mean and end to all things — God.

PHILIP JAMES BAILEY

SEPTEMBER 11

I shall pass through this world but once. Any good thing therefore that I can do, or any kindness I can show to any human being, let me do it now. Let me not defer nor neglect it, for I shall not pass this way again.

Nobody is sure who wrote this. It is well known but it always moves me. My failures in kindness, the help I did not offer, give me much regret.

Change doesn't cause pain: resistance to change is what causes pain.

SEPTEMBER 12

ANONYMOUS

The poet James Montgomery found inspiration in the sunflower.

SEPTEMBER 13

Eagle of flowers! I see thee stand,
And on the sun's noon glory gaze:
With eye like his, thy lids expand
And fringe their disk with golden rays:
Though fixed on earth, in darkness rooted there,
Light is thine element, thy dwelling air,
Thy prospect heaven.

So would mine eagle-soul descry,
Beyond the path where planets run,
The light of immortality,
The splendour of creation's sun:
Though sprung from earth, and hastening to the tomb,
I hope a flower of paradise to bloom,
I look to heaven.

On Lebanon His cedars stand,
Trees full of sap, works of His hand;
In them the birds their cabins dight,
The fir tree is the stork's delight.
The wild goat on the hills, in cells
Of rock the hermit coney dwells.
How full of creatures is the earth,
To which Thy wisdom gave their birth!
And those that in the wide sea breed
The bounds of number far exceed;
There the huge whales with finny feet
Dance underneath the sailing fleet.
God's glory shall for ever stay,
He shall with joy his works survey.

The idea of whales dancing below the waves delights me. This version of Psalm 51 by Thomas Carew is full of joyful wonder.

With ills unending strives the putter-off.

A funny maxim by Hesiod, one of the earliest poets of ancient Greece.

SEPTEMBER

I think what we call the dullness of things is a disease in ourselves.

I like this thought from George Eliot. Boredom has little to do with circumstances: everything to do with our response to them.

> Despair is not for good or wise,
> And should not be for love;
> We all must bear our destinies,
> And bend to those above.
> Birds flying o'er the stormy seas
> Alight upon their proper trees,
> Yet wisest men not always know
> Where they should stop or whither go.

Walter Savage Landor's lines are about accepting our destiny. It is only in acceptance of events and people that we can find serenity.

> To live in great simplicity is exceeding wise.
>
> ST PACHOMIUS

> How much soe'er I sin, whate'er I do
> Of evil, still the sky above is blue,
> The stars look down in beauty as before:
> It is enough to walk as best we may,
> To walk and sighing dream of that blest day
> When ill we cannot quell shall be no more.

Sometimes we cannot change ourselves, much as we would like to. Arthur Hugh Clough says that it is enough we do our best in life.

SEPTEMBER 20   Live out your life as a happy child of God in the sunshine of His love.

This advice, so obvious that it has taken me years to understand it, came from Father Mowbray Smith, a man of great simplicity.

SEPTEMBER 21

Time that is past, thou never canst recall;
Of time to come, thou art not sure at all;
Time present, only, is within thy power:
Now, now improve, then, whilst thou canst, the hour.

This verse by John Byrom says that we should try to live in the day, not letting the past grieve us or the future dismay us.

SEPTEMBER 22   If a man sees that his companion hates him, he shall love him the more. For the community of the living is the carriage of God's majesty, and where there is a rent in the carriage, one must fill it, and where there is so little love that the joining comes apart, one must love more on one's own side to overcome the lack.

RABBI RAFAEL

SEPTEMBER 23

One, two, whatever you do,
Start it well and carry it through.
Try, try, never say die,
Things will come right,
You know, by and by.

The simplicity of this anonymous children's rhyme is what appeals to me. The sing-song verse is full of comforting sense.

He who has begun his task, has half done it. Have the courage SEPTEMBER 24
to be wise.

*This saying of the Roman poet, Horace, is a useful one for those
moments when my heart fails me and I want to give up struggling.*

What is this life if, full of care, SEPTEMBER 25
We have no time to stand and stare.

No time to stand beneath the
   boughs
And stare as long as sheep
   or cows.

No time to see, when
   woods we pass,
Where squirrels hide
   their nuts in grass.

No time to see, in
   broad daylight,
Streams full of stars,
   like skies at night.

A poor life this if, full of
   care,
We have no time to stand
   and stare.

W.H. DAVIES

SEPTEMBER 26

We cannot kindle when we will
The fire which in the heart resides;
The spirit bloweth and is still,
In mystery our soul abides.
But tasks in hours of insight willed
Can be through hours of gloom fulfilled.

With aching hands and bleeding feet
We dig and heap, lay stone on stone;
We bear the burden and the heat
Of the long day, and wish 'twere done.
Not till the hours of light return
All we have built do we discern.

MATTHEW ARNOLD

SEPTEMBER 27   He who sows courtesy, reaps friendship, and he who sows kindness, gathers love.

ST BASIL

SEPTEMBER

To know what you prefer, instead of saying Amen to what the world tells you you ought to prefer, is to have kept your soul alive.

ROBERT LOUIS STEVENSON

For me this poem by Francis Bret Harte has reassurance. There may *be more meaning in the small things of life than I can see.*

> Came the relief. 'What, sentry, ho!
> How passed the night through thy long waking?'
> 'Cold, cheerless, dark, – as may befit
> The hour before the dawn is breaking.'
>
> 'No sight? no sound?' 'No; nothing save
> The plover from the marshes calling,
> And in yon Western sky, about
> An hour ago, a star was falling.'
>
> 'A star? There's nothing strange in that.'
> 'No, nothing; but, above the thicket,
> Somehow it seemed to me that God
> Somewhere had just relieved a picket.'

A man should never be ashamed to own that he has been in the wrong, which is but saying in other words that he is wiser today than he was yesterday.

Sensible words from Alexander Pope. Hard though it is to admit to error, if I do so, my mistakes or wrongdoings become no great matter. And the reward is to enjoy happier relationships.

OCTOBER

Me it delights in mellow autumn tide
To mark the pleasaunce that mine eyes surrounds —
The forest trees like coloured posies pied,
The uplands mealy grey and russet grounds —
Seeking for joy where joyance most abounds;
Not found, I ween, in courts and halls of pride,
Where folly feeds on flattery's sights and sounds
And with sick heart but seemeth to be merry.
True pleasaunce is with humble food supplied,
Like shepherd swain who plucks the bramble berry
With savoury appetite from hedgerow briars,
Then drops content by molehill's sunny side;
Proving thereby low joys and small desires
Are easiest fed and soonest satisfied.

Now is the time of dazzling autumn. I love John Clare's 'low joys and small desires'. Joy in small things is the secret of content.

There is an idea abroad among moral people that they should make their neighbours good. One person I have to make good: myself. But my duty to my neighbour is much more nearly expressed by saying that I have to make him happy if I may.

An acute perception by Robert Louis Stevenson. I have to mind my own business about others — neither judge nor try to improve them. Only by accepting them as they are, can I make them happy.

OCTOBER 3   If time be of all things the most precious, wasting time must be the greatest prodigality, since lost time is never found again. Let us then up and be doing.

BENJAMIN FRANKLIN

OCTOBER 4   *Today is the feast day of St Francis, the saint who acknowledged kinship with all creation. He was so gentle-hearted that he would pick worms off the road so that they wouldn't be crushed. Here is John Galsworthy's prayer for gentleness to all creatures.*

> To all the humble beasts there be,
> To all the birds on land and sea,
> Great Spirit! sweet protection give,
> That free and happy they may live!
>
> And to our hearts the rapture bring
> Of love for every living thing;
> Make of us all one kin, and bless
> Our ways with Christ's own gentleness.

Build not on tomorrow,
But seize on today!
From no future borrow,
The present to pay.

Forbode not new sorrow –
Bear that of today,
And trust that the morrow
Shall chase it away.

I was delighted to find this poem by Henry David Thoreau. Poets tell us frequently, and I seem to need reminding of it often, that only the present time is ours. I must live just twenty-four hours at a time.

Certainly it is heaven upon earth to have a man's mind move in charity, rest in providence, and turn upon the poles of truth.

FRANCIS BACON

When changes in the world around me or in my own life upset me, I try to remember these lines of Alfred, Lord Tennyson.

The old order changeth, yielding place to new,
And God fulfils himself in many ways,
Lest one good custom should corrupt the world.
Comfort thyself.

Be a friend to thyself, and others will befriend thee.

PROVERB

OCTOBER 9   A kind word with forgiveness is better than charity followed by insult.

THE KORAN

OCTOBER 10   *I try to start my day with a little meditation. If I remember it, the day seems less rushed, as this anonymous verse points out.*

> I got up early one morning and rushed right into the day;
> I had so much to accomplish that I didn't have time to pray.
> Problems just tumbled about me, and heavier came each task.
> 'Why doesn't God help me?' I wondered. He answered: 'You didn't ask.'
> I woke up early this morning, and paused before starting the day.
> I had so much to accomplish, that I had to take time to pray.

OCTOBER 11   *When I was searching for God, I had help from André Geraghty, who had once been a street drunk and had changed into a sober man. Reminding me of life's many blessings, he used to say:*

And where there is a gift, sure there must be a Giver.

OCTOBER 12   A man is made by his belief.
As he believes, so he is.

If we change our thinking (and with effort we can), we can alter our lives. So says the Bhagavad-Gita, *the Hindu classic text.*

If you don't make mistakes, you don't make anything.   OCTOBER 13

AUTHOR UNKNOWN

William Wordsworth, looking at a kitten playing with a leaf and his   OCTOBER 14
baby watching it, wished that he could lead his life like theirs.

> Now and then I may possess
> Hours of perfect gladsomeness,
> – Pleased by any random toy:
> By a kitten's busy joy,
> Or an infant's laughing eye
> Sharing in the ecstasy;
> I would fare like that or this,
> Find my wisdom in my bliss;
> Keep the sprightly soul awake,
> And have faculties to take,
> Even from things by sorrow wrought,
> Matter for a jocund thought,
> Spite of care, and spite of grief,
> To gambol with Life's falling leaf.

OCTOBER 15   I cannot close my eyes upon this day without setting down some record of it; yet the foolish insufficiency of words! At sunset I stood in the meadow above my house and watched the red orb sink into purple mist, whilst in the violet heaven behind me rose the perfect moon. Never, I could fancy, did autumn clothe in such magnificence the elms and birches; never, I should think, did the leafage on my walls blaze in such royal crimson. Was it for five minutes, or was it for an hour that I watched the yellow butterfly wafted as if by an insensible tremor of air amid the garden glintings? In every autumn there comes one such flawless day.

GEORGE GISSING

OCTOBER 16

Make new friends
But keep the old.
One is silver,
The other gold.

AUTHOR UNKNOWN

I'll not willingly offend,
Nor be easily offended;
What's amiss I'll strive to mend,
And endure what can't be mended.

ISAAC WATTS

If the stars should appear one night in a thousand years, how would men believe and adore; and preserve for many generations the remembrance of the city of God which had been shown! But every night come out these envoys of beauty, and light the universe with their admonishing smile.

RALPH WALDO EMERSON

Cease to lament for that thou canst not help
    And study help for that which thou lamentest.
    Why, courage then: what cannot be avoided
    'Twere childish weakness to lament or fear.
    What's gone and what's past help
    Should be past grief.

WILLIAM SHAKESPEARE

The kingdom of God is within you.

These are the words of Jesus. Though they are familiar to millions, I find them thought-provoking. If I must look within for God's kingdom, the responsibility for finding it is mine.

OCTOBER 21

Grow old along with me!
The best is yet to be,
The last of life, for which the first was made:
Our times are in His hand
Who saith: 'A whole I planned,
Youth shows but half; trust God: see all nor be afraid!'

ROBERT BROWNING

OCTOBER 22

'Where can there ever be a start when everyone's involved in the mess, and everyone affects everyone else?' The answer is 'Don't calculate'. The upshot, in time or eternity, is out of our hands. We know that, involved though we are, we can make a start under grace, any moment and every moment ourselves. Nothing else should concern us.

VICTOR GOLLANCZ

OCTOBER 23

This verse is embroidered on an eighteenth-century sampler. The joy of learning, of books, or of poetry, outlasts mere possessions.

Look well to what you have in hand,
For larning is better than house and land,
When land is gone and money spent,
Then larning is most excellent.

OCTOBER 24

Many men owe the grandeur of their lives to their tremendous difficulties.

CHARLES HADDON SPURGEON

For to Him who is everywhere men come not by travelling but by loving.

This is was written by St Augustine. Sometimes we think that a geographical change will solve our problems. It rarely does.

John Addington Symonds wrote this poem about chrysanthemums.

Latecomers! Ye, when autumn's wealth is past;
When pale October strips the yellowing leaves;
When on our garden lawns and dripping
    eaves
The rain-soaked foliage of the elm is cast.
When 'neath grey skies the wild Atlantic
    blast
Searches the flowerbed for each bloom
    that cleaves
To blackening tendrils; when
    November weaves
Fretwork of frost, and winter frowns
    at last;
Ye, in the year's decay and death of
    hope,
Dawn with your hues auroral, hues of
    rose,
Saffron and ivory, amber, amethyst;
More delicate, more dear, more true than
    those
Gay blossoms which July sunbeam kissed,
Purer of scent than honey heliotrope.

My friendly fire, thou blazest clear and bright,
Nor smoke nor ashes soil thy grateful flame;
Thy temperate splendour cheers the gloom of night,
Thy genial heat enlivens the chilled frame.
I love to muse me o'er the evening hearth,
I love to pause in meditation's sway;
And whilst each object gives reflection birth,
Mark thy brisk rise, and see thy slow decay:
And I would wish, like thee, to shine serene,
Like thee, within mine influence, all to cheer;
And wish at last, in life's declining scene,
As I had beamed as bright, to fade as clear:

ROBERT SOUTHEY

Till you love men so as to desire their happiness, with a thirst
equal to the zeal of your own; till you delight in God for being
good to all; you never enjoy the world.

THOMAS TRAHERNE

On my friendships I practise no art, except to love utterly, to feign nothing, to hide nothing, and in a word to pour out everything into my friend's ears, just as it comes from my heart.

FRANCESCO PETRARCH

Lord, many times I am aweary quite
Of mine own self, my sin, my vanity —
Yet be not Thou, or I am lost outright,
Weary of me.

And hate against myself I often bear,
And enter with myself in fierce debate;
Take Thou my part against myself, nor share
In that just hate.

This poem by Richard Chenevix Trench is for all self-haters. In such moods I try to remember that God hates nothing that He has made. He loves us unconditionally, demanding nothing in return.

When I found these words, I was mourning the death of my father. We didn't always get on, yet I miss him terribly. I do not know who wrote this but it is a help this Hallowe'en. It comforts me to hope there is a possibility we might meet in the next life.

We do not love in vain. So surely as we must live, having lived, so must we love, having loved. And after some term, longer and or shorter, but a mere vibration of the great pendulum of eternity, we shall all be reunited.

NOVEMBER

Teach me to listen, Lord,
to those nearest to me
my family, my friends, my co-workers.
Help me to be aware that
no matter what words I hear,
their message is,
'Accept the person I am. Listen to me.'

Teach me to listen, Lord,
to myself.
Help me to be less afraid,
to trust the voice inside —
in the deepest part of me.

Teach me to listen, Lord,
for Your voice —
in busyness and in boredom,
in certainty and in doubt,
in noise and in silence

AUTHOR UNKNOWN

We should impart our courage, and not our despair, our health
and ease, and not our disease, and take care that this does not
spread by contagion.

HENRY DAVID THOREAU

NOVEMBER

NOVEMBER 3   *These rather mysterious lines by Walt Whitman remind me to stop comparing myself with others. I must accept my own path.*

> I lead no man to a dinner-table, library, exchange
> But each man and each woman of you I lead upon a knoll,
> My left hand hooking you round the waist,
> My right hand pointing to landscapes of continents and the
>   public road.
> Not I, not any one else can travel that road for you,
> You must travel it for yourself.
>
> It is not far, it is within reach,
> Perhaps you have been on it since you were born and did not
>   know ...

NOVEMBER 4   To accomplish things, there must first be an idea that the things are possible; then the watchword must be to try. Failures, so called, are but fingerposts pointing out the right direction to those who are willing to learn.

THOMAS A. EDISON

NOVEMBER

Best be yourself, imperial, plain and true.

NOVEMBER 5

ROBERT BROWNING

One ought every day at least to hear a little song, read a good poem, see a fine picture, and, if possible, speak a few reasonable words.

NOVEMBER 6

Acquire a routine of using each day well, says Johann Goethe.

I asked for peace —
My sins arose,
And bound me close,
I could not find release.

NOVEMBER 7

I asked for truth —
My doubts came in,
And with their din
They wearied all my youth.

I asked for love —
My lovers failed,
And griefs assailed
Around, beneath, above.

I asked for Thee —
And Thou didst come
To take me home
Within Thy heart to be.

This poem was written by Digby Dolben, who died at twenty-nine.

NOVEMBER 8   *These lines by William Wordsworth are about accepting our own shortcomings, acknowledging that they may be a saving grace.*

> How strange, that all
> The terrors, pains, and early miseries,
> Regrets, vexations, lassitudes interfused
> Within my mind, should e'er have born a part,
> And that a needful part, in making up
> The calm existence that is mine when I
> Am worthy of myself.

NOVEMBER 9   Herein is love, not that we loved God, but that he loved us ...

This message from the First Epistle of St John has often eluded me. What matters is that I should believe, accept and feel that God loves me. Whether I love God is much less important, almost irrelevant perhaps. From feeling He loves me, so much springs.

NOVEMBER 10   Cheerfulness keeps up a kind of daylight in the mind, filling it with a steady and perpetual serenity.

JOSEPH ADDISON

NOVEMBER 11   *Today is the day when peace was signed after the First World War. Thomas à Kempis has this to say about personal peace.*

We might have much peace, if we would not meddle with other men's sayings and doings, that belong not to us. How may he long live in peace, that wilfully will meddle with other men's business?

E'er you remark another's sin
Bid your conscience look within.

BENJAMIN FRANKLIN

Sidney Smith wrote a list of cures for low spirits. It includes:

Amusing books.
Short views of human life — no further than dinner or tea.
Be as busy as you can.
See as much as you can of those friends who respect and like
    you.
And of those acquaintances who amuse you.
Make no secret of low spirits to your friends, but talk of them
    freely — they are always worse for dignified concealment.
Make the room where you commonly sit gay and pleasant.
Don't be too severe upon yourself, or underrate yourself, but do
    yourself justice.
Keep good blazing fires.

NOVEMBER 14 It is worth a thousand pounds a year to have the habit of looking on the bright side of things.

SAMUEL JOHNSON

NOVEMBER 15 *This poem by Geoffrey Studdert-Kennedy is about God in the factories, in mines, in steel works. He is there in offices too.*

> When through the night the furnace fires a-flaring,
> Shooting out tongues of flame like leaping blood,
> Speak to the heart of Love, alive and daring,
> Sing of the boundless energy of God.
>
> When in the depths the patient miner striving
> Feels in his arm the vigour of the Lord,
> Strikes for a kingdom and his King's arriving,
> Holding his pick more splendid than the sword.
>
> Then will he come with meekness for his glory,
> God in a workman's jacket as before,
> Living again the eternal story,
> Sweeping the shavings from his workshop floor.

NOVEMBER

Whatever harm a hater may do to a hater, or an enemy do to an enemy, a wrongly directed mind will do even greater mischief. Whatever good a mother, or a father, or some other family relative will do, a well-directed mind will do us even greater service.

NOVEMBER 16

This saying is adapted from the Dhammapada, an anthology of Buddhist devotion, which dates back to the first century BC.

Why should we fear that which we cannot fly?
Fear is more pain than is the pain it fears.

NOVEMBER 17

These two lines come from a sonnet about death by Sir Philip Sidney. When I am fearful in advance about some ordeal I simply add the pain of fear to the pain on the way, suffering twice over.

I used to find it almost impossible to pray. I thought I had to do it in a particular way, using particular words, and thinking only particular thoughts. Then I found the courage to break these rules thanks to this advice. I don't know who originally said it.

NOVEMBER 18

Pray how you can, not how you can't.

Mortals that would follow me
Love Virtue, she alone is free.
She can teach you how to climb
Higher than the sphery chime;
Or if Virtue feeble were,
Heaven itself would stoop to her.

NOVEMBER 19

JOHN MILTON

NOVEMBER 20

Teach me to feel another's woe,
To hide the fault I see,
That mercy I to others show
That mercy show to me.

ALEXANDER POPE

NOVEMBER 21

Why should I hasten to solve every riddle which life offers me? I am well assured that the Questioner, who brings me so many problems, will bring the answers also in due time.

RALPH WALDO EMERSON

NOVEMBER 22

For the day of St Cecilia, music's patron saint, I have found some lines by a doctor-poet, John Armstrong. Music for me has a power to heal and I need reminding of this source of calm.

There is a charm, a power that sways the breast;
Bids every passion revel or be still;
Inspires with rage, or all your cares dissolves;
Can sooth distraction and almost despair.
That power is music.

NOVEMBER 23

Be thou what thou singly art, and personate only thy self. Swim smoothly in the stream of thy nature, and live but one man.

Advice from Sir Thomas Browne, the seventeenth-century writer. Only by being true to myself can I avoid lying, people-pleasing and insincerity. Self-acceptance and self-love is the key.

NOVEMBER

The decisive heart-searching is the beginning of the way in a man's life; it is, again and again, the beginning of a human way. But heart-searching is decisive only if it leads to the way. For there is a sterile kind of heart-searching which leads to nothing but self-torture, despair and still deeper enmeshment.

NOVEMBER 24

MARTIN BUBER

NOVEMBER 25

Three centuries ago Bishop Thomas Ken wrote a hymnbook for Winchester College. These two verses appeal to me, because sometimes I lie awake tormented by worries and gloomy thoughts.

When in the night I sleepless lie,
My soul with heavenly thoughts
   supply;
Let no ill dreams disturb my rest,
No power of darkness me molest.

O may my Guardian while I sleep
Close to my bed his vigils keep,
His love angelical instil,
Stop all avenues of ill.

NOVEMBER 26   *I underestimate the value of cosiness, the humble pleasure of a warm home and comfy chair — which is why I enjoy these lines by John Collins. They remind me not to take such things for granted.*

> In the downhill of life when I find I'm declining,
> May my fate no less fortunate be,
> Than a snug elbow chair will afford for reclining,
> And a cot that o'erlooks the wide sea;
> With a porch at my door, both for shelter and
> shade, too,
>
> As the sunshine or rain may prevail;
> And a small spot of ground for the use of the
> spade, too,
> With a barn for the use of the flail.
> A cow for my dairy, a dog for my game,
> And a purse when a friend wants to borrow,
> I'll envy no nabob his riches or fame,
> Or what honours may wait him tomorrow.

Our greatest glory is not in never falling, but in rising every time we fall.

CONFUCIUS

NOVEMBER 27

Marcus Aurelius was Emperor of Rome and also a philosopher. His writings still have lessons for us today. Here he reminds us about the wisdom of living a day at a time, in the present only.

NOVEMBER 28

Do not take your whole life into your head at a time, nor burden yourself with the weight of the future. Neither what is past nor what is to come need afflict you, for you have only to deal with the present; and this is strangely lessened if you take it singly and by itself.

There is a verse by Giles Fletcher that fills me not only with comfort but also a sense of spiritual awe. We do not have to struggle alone against our difficulties. What I cannot do, He can.

NOVEMBER 29

> He is a path, if any be misled;
> He is a robe, if any naked be;
> If any chance to hunger, He is bread;
> If any be a bondman, He is free;
> If any be but weak, how strong is He;
> To dead men, life He is; to sick men, health;
> To blind men, sight; and to the needy, wealth;
> A pleasure without loss; a treasure without stealth.

Every man is said to have his particular ambition. Whether it be true, or not, I cannot say; but I can say that I have one: that of being truly esteemed of my fellow men, by rendering myself worthy of their esteem.

ABRAHAM LINCOLN

NOVEMBER 30

DECEMBER

There are moments of serenity for most of us within easy reach — if we turn our eyes upwards to the sky. William Wordsworth describes the calm inspiration of stars or a coming night storm.

> I would walk alone
> Under the quiet stars, and at that time
> Have felt whate'er there is of power in sound
> To breathe an elevated mood, by form
> Or image unprofaned; and I would stand,
> If the night blackened with a coming storm,
> Beneath some rock, listening to notes that are
> The ghostly language of the ancient earth,
> Or make their dim abode in distant winds.
> Thence did I drink the visionary power;
> And deem not profitless those fleeting moods
> Of shadowy exultation.

You want your life to be different, you want to rise above humdrum routine. You want to render a real service. You can have it different, but you do not need to change your job in order to change your life. Just change yourself. Change your thoughts and attitudes. Become enthusiastic and the old job will become a new one, and your life will fill up with power.

One way to banish boredom and self-pity is to make a conscious attempt to be enthusiastic, says Norman Vincent Peale. It works.

Then said a rich man, Speak to us of Giving. And he
answered:

You give but little when you give of your possessions.

It is when you give of yourself that you truly give.

For what are your possessions but things you keep and
guard for fear you may need them tomorrow?

And tomorrow, what shall tomorrow bring to the over-
prudent dog burying bones in the trackless sand as he
follows the pilgrims to the holy city?

And what is fear of need but need itself?

Is not dread of thirst when your well is full, the thirst that
is unquenchable?

There are those who give little of the much which they
have – and they give it for recognition and their hidden
desire makes their gifts unwholesome.

And there are those who have little and give it all.

These are the believers of life and the bounty of life, and
their coffer is never empty.

KALIL GIBRAN

I should not like to change places with our father, Abraham! What good would it do God if Abraham became like blind Bunam and blind Bunam became like Abraham? Rather than have this happen, I think I shall try to become a little more myself.

RABBI BUNAM

No pitted toad behind a stone
But hoards some secret grace;
The meanest slug with midnight gone
Has left a silver trace.

No dullest eyes to beauty blind,
Uplifted to the beast,
But prove some kin with angel kind,
Though lowliest and least.

RALPH HODGSON

If God bears with the worst of us, we may surely endure each other.

SIR WALTER SCOTT

Life, believe, is not the dream
So dark, as sages say;
Oft a little morning rain
Foretells a pleasant day.

ANNE BRONTË

DECEMBER 8

It is wicked to grow accustomed to good things.

AUTHOR UNKNOWN

DECEMBER 9

These lines come from an old Elizabethan parchment. The poet Robert Southey liked and kept them in his commonplace book.

Have compassion tenderlye.
Doe goode deeds lustilye.
Love hertelye.
Love faithfullye.
Love God onlye.
Love all others for him charitablye.
Love in adversitye.
Love in prosperitye.
Think always on love, which is nothinge but
 God himself.
Thus love bringeth the lover to love, which is
 God himself.

DECEMBER 10

All that we are is the result of what we have thought.

BUDDHA

DECEMBER 11

How beautiful it is to be alive!
To wake each morn as if the Maker's grace
Did us afresh from nothingness derive,
That we might sing 'How happy is our case!
How beautiful it is to be alive.'

HENRY SEPTIMUS SUTTON

What is more tender than a mother's love
To the sweet infant fondling in her arms?
What arguments need her compassion move
To hear its cries, and help it in its harms?
Now if the tenderest mother were possessed
Of all the love within her single breast,
Of all the mothers since the world began,
'Tis nothing to the love of God to man.

JOHN BYROM

DECEMBER 12

Of all the old festivals that of
Christmas awakens the strongest and
most heartfelt associations. The services of
the church about this season are
extremely tender and inspiring. I do not
know a grander effect of music on the
moral feelings than to hear the full choir
and pealing organ performing a
Christmas anthem.

DECEMBER 13

*Washington Irving reminds us
to enjoy the music of
Christmas. I do not think it is
necessary to be a Christian to
join in. It is a time, I hope, when even atheists can
enjoy singing carols.*

DECEMBER 14

The embers of the day are red
Beyond the murky hill.
The kitchen smokes: the bed
In the darkling house is spread:
The great sky darkens overhead,
And the great woods are shrill.
So far have I been led,
Lord, by Thy will:
So far I have followed, Lord, and wondered still.

The breeze from the enbalmèd land
Blows sudden toward the shore,
And claps my cottage door.
I hear the signal, Lord – I understand.
The night at Thy command
Comes. I will eat and sleep and will not
    question more.

*This lovely poem by
Robert Louis
Stevenson is about
serene acceptance
at the end of
the day. Lord,
help me to
that
acceptance.*

DECEMBER

Inner peace requires the ability to let go of anxieties, including worries about others as well as oneself, says Bishop Joseph Hall.

He that taketh his own cares upon himself loads himself in vain with an uneasy burden. The fear of what may come, expectation of what will come, desire of what will not come and inability of redressing all these, must need breed in him continual torment. I will cast my cares upon God: they cannot hurt Him.

The long day wanes: the slow moon climbs: the deep
Moans round with many voices. Come, my friends,
'Tis not too late to seek a newer world ...
Though much is taken, much abides; and though
We are not now that strength which in old days
Moved earth and heaven; that which we are, we are:
One equal temper of heroic hearts
Made weak by time and fate, but strong in will
To strive, to seek, to find and not to yield.

In this passage, Alfred, Lord Tennyson tells us that it is not too late to seek renewal. Age should never prevent me from setting out on a new inner journey. I find the last line particularly inspiring.

Every year I live I am more convinced that the waste of life lies in the love we have not given, the powers we have not used, the selfish prudence that will risk nothing, and which, shirking pain, misses happiness as well.

MARY CHOLMONDELEY

DECEMBER 18

Whate'er we leave to God, God does,
And blesses us;
The work we choose should be our own,
God lets alone.

Henry David Thoreau is writing about handing over our work to God. If I can let go of my own life and let God in, He comes in. When I keep Him out, determined to do it all myself, He stays out.

DECEMBER 19

Courage grows by doing; fear grows by failing to do.

AUTHOR UNKNOWN

DECEMBER 20

Was it a fancy, bred of vagrant guess,
Or well-remembered fact, that He was born
When half the world was wint'ry and forlorn,
In nature's utmost season of distress?
So be it: for in truth 'tis ever so,
That when the winter of the soul is bare,
The seed of heaven first begins to grow,
Peeping abroad in desert of despair.

When we are at rock bottom God helps us, says Hartley Coleridge.

DECEMBER 21

We should strive to celebrate the true meaning of Christmas, says Charles Dickens — the love of friends, family, neighbours and God.

Whatever else be lost among the years, let us keep Christmas; its meaning never ends. Whatever doubt assail us, or what fear, let us hold close this day, remembering friends.

DECEMBER

DECEMBER 22

As a thought for the shortest day in the year, there is this poem by Walter de la Mare about birds singing through the cold winter.

I know not what small winter birds these are,
Warbling their hearts out in that dusky glade
While the pale lustre of the morning star
In heaven begins to fade.

Not me they sing for, this — earth's shortest — day,
A human listening at his window-glass;
They would, affrighted, cease and flit away
At glimpse even of my face.

And yet how strangely mine their music seems,
As if of all things loved my heart was heir,
Had helped create them — albeit in my dreams —
And they disdained my share.

DECEMBER 23

There cannot be too much joy.

BENEDICT DE SPINOZA

There may be meaning even for atheists in the tale of a God who became a baby. Thomas Traherne tells us to become likewise.

Our Saviour's meaning when He said, 'He must be born again and become a little child, that will enter into the kingdom of heaven' is deeper far than is generally believed. It is not only in a careless reliance upon divine providence that we are to become little children, or in the feebleness and shortness of our anger, and simplicity of our passions; but in the peace and purity of all our soul. Which purity also is a deeper thing than is commonly apprehended; for we must disrobe ourselves of all false colours, and unclothe our souls of evil habits; all our thoughts must be infant-like and clear, the powers of our soul free from the leaven of this world, and disentangled from men's conceits and customs. Grit in the eye or yellow jaundice will not let man see those objects truly that are before it. And therefore it is requisite that we should be as very strangers to thoughts, customs and opinions of men in this world, as if we were but little children.

When the time of that blessed birth was come, God's Son of heaven, so going out of that womb without travail or sorrow, suddenly was upon hay at His mother's feet. And anon she, devoutly inclined, with sovereign joy took Him in her arms, and sweetly embracing and kissing, laid Him in her bosom, and with a full breast, as she was taught of the Holy Ghost, washed him all about with her sweet milk, and so wrapped Him in the kerchief of her head, and laid him in the crèche. And anon the ox and the ass, kneeling down, laid their mouths on the crèche, breathing through their noses upon the child as if they knew by reason that in that cold time the child so simply covered had need to be heated in that manner.

I adapted this touching passage from The Mirror of the Blessed Life of Jesu Christ *by Nicholas Love, written nearly six centuries ago. What moves me in the story are the details − the young mother breastfeeding her baby, then wrapping Him in her scarf, and the beasts breathing over the manger to keep the child warm.*

The life of the child born at Christmas time was the life of a victor not victim. For this baby, as the poet Mary Coleridge points out, is the child that challenges and destroys the world's values.

> I saw a stable, low and very bare,
> A little child in a manger.
> The oxen knew Him, had Him in their care,
> To men He was a stranger.
> The safety of the world was lying there,
> And the world's danger.

DECEMBER 27   By no means, however, can it be our true task in the world into which we have been set, to turn away from the things and beings that we meet on our way and that attract our hearts; our task is precisely to get in touch, by hallowing our relationship with them, with what manifests itself in them as beauty, pleasure, enjoyment ... Rejoicing in the world, if we hallow it with our whole being, leads to rejoicing in God.

MARTIN BUBER

DECEMBER 28   *The old carols were never glum. Most of them had a great sense of the mystery of the God who became a child combined with an innocent enjoyment of the winter feast — like this one.*

> Lift up your heartës and be glad!
> In Christës birth the angels bade;
> Say each to other if any be sad,
> What cheer? Good cheer! Good cheer! Good cheer!
> Be merry and glad this New Year.
>
> Now the King of Heaven his birth hath take,
> Joy and mirth we ought to make,
> Say to each other for His sake,
> What cheer? Good cheer! Good cheer! Good cheer!
> Be merry and glad this New Year.

DECEMBER 29   He is a wise man who does not grieve for the things he has not, but rejoices for those which he has.

EPICTETUS

DECEMBER

Ned Farmer was a nineteenth-century railway worker who published a book of poems. He was not a very good poet but one of his verses has a simple message which I find appealing. Here it is:

> I'm fond of old maxims, they serve to convey,
> A vast deal of truth in a very brief way.
> For instance, take this one, which none can deny.
> It's wonderful what we can do if we try!

All below heaven changes; spring, summer, autumn, each has its turn. The fortunes of the world change; what was high, lies low; what was low, rises high. Riches take wing and flee away; bereavements happen. Friends become enemies and enemies friends. Our wishes, aims and plans change. There is nothing stable but Thou, O my God! And Thou art the centre and life of all who change, who trust Thee as their Father, who look to Thee, and who are content to put themselves into Thy hands.

JOHN HENRY NEWMAN

ACKNOWLEDGEMENTS

I have tried to obtain permission from copyright holders to reproduce the quotations in this book, but there are some I could not trace. The publishers will be happy to rectify any omissions in future editions. I should like to thank the following for permission to reprint:

The Anglican Book Centre and Darton, Longman and Todd Ltd, UK, for extracts from *God of Surprises* by Gerard W. Hughes, published in Canada by the Anglican Book Centre, 1986.

The Estate of Martin Buber, c/o Balkin Agency, Amherst, Massachusetts, for an extract from *The Legend of Baal Shem* by Martin Buber, published by East and West Library, Horovitz, London, 1956 and Harper Bros, New York, 1955.

Bear and Company, for extracts from *Original Blessing* by Matthew Fox, copyright Bear and Co Inc. 1983 by permission of Bear and Co. Inc., PO Box 2860, Santa Fé, NM 87504.

Rabbi Lionel Blue and The Universe, UK, for the story of St Walston by Rabbi Lionel Blue.

Carol Publishing Group and International Thomson Publishing Services Ltd, for extracts from *The Way of Man, According to the Teachings of the Hasidism* by Martin Buber, copyright © 1966 by The Citadel Press, published by arrangement with Carol Publishing Group; published in Britain by Routledge and Kegan Paul Ltd, London, 1950.

Curtis Brown Ltd for extracts from *The Wisdom of Laotse*, translated by Lin Yutang, Michael Joseph Ltd, reproduced by permission of Curtis Brown Ltd, London, © 1948 Random House Inc.

J.M.Dent and Sons Ltd, for extracts from *Jewish Mysticism* by Martin Buber, J.M.Dent and Sons Ltd, London 1931.

Faber and Faber Ltd for an extract from *Diary of a Russian Priest* by Alexander Elchaninov, Faber and Faber Ltd, London.

Victor Gollancz Ltd, for extracts from *More for Timothy*, by Victor Gollancz.

Harper Collins Publishers Ltd and Templegate for an extract from *Tensions* by Harry Williams; Harry Williams and Templegate for an extract from *The Joy of God* by Harry Williams.

Harper Collins Publishers Ltd for an extract from *The Sword in the Stone*, by T.H.White, published by Harper Collins Publishers Ltd and an extract from *A Gift from God* by Mother Teresa of Calcutta, Collins Ltd.

Harvard University Press for the use of Emily Dickinson's poems in this book and also in *The Yearbook of Hope and Inspiration* and in *The Yearbook of Comfort and Joy*. Poetry is reprinted by permission of the publishers and the Trustees of Amherst College from *The Poems of Emily Dickinson*, Thomas H. Johnson, ed., Cambridge Massachusetts; The Bellknap Press of Harvard University Press, copyright © 1951, 1955, 1979, 1983 by the President and Fellows of Harvard College, and from *The Complete Poems of Emily Dickinson*, edited by Thomas H. Johnson, copyright © 1929, 1935 by Martha Dickinson Bianchi; copyright © renewed 1957, 1963 by Mary L. Hampson: Little, Brown and Company, Boston.

The Literary Trustees of Walter de la Mare, and The Society of Authors as their representative for permission to quote 'A Rose in Water' and 'Birds in Winter' by Walter de la Mare.

Macmillan London Ltd, for *The Mystery*, *Lines*, and lines from *Flying Scrolls*, by Ralph Hodgson.

Al-Hafiz B.A. Masri for an extract from *Animals in Islam* by Al-Hafiz B.A. Masri, Athene Trust, 20 Lavant St, Petersfield, Hants.

John Murray (Publishers) Ltd for an extract from *The Book of Lieh Tzu* by A.G.Graham and an extract from *Safety First* by Mary Cholmondeley.

Pavilion Books Ltd and Workman Publishing Co for an extract from *All I Need to Know I Learned from my Cat* by Suzy Becker, copyright © 1990 by Suzanne Becker, reprinted with permission of Workman Publishing Co and Pavilion Books Ltd.

Penguin Books Ltd for extracts from *The Koran* translated by N.J.Dawood (Penguin Classics, Fifth Edition, 1990), copyright © N.J.Dawood 1956, 1959, 1966, 1968, 1974, 1990.

Oxford University Press for extracts from *Centuries, Poems and Thanksgivings*, by Thomas Traherne, ed H.M. Margoliouth, Oxford University Press, 1958.

Reform Synagogues of Great Britain for 'When All Within is Dark' by Israel Abrahams, from *Forms of Prayer for Jewish Worship: Daily, Sabbath and Occasional Prayers*, The Reform Synagogues of Great Britain, London 1977.

Random House Inc. for extracts from *Tales of the Hasidim* by Martin Buber, copyright © 1947, 1948 and renewed 1975 by Schocken Books Inc. Reprinted by permission of Pantheon Books, a division of Random House, Inc.; also for an extract from *The Prophet* by Kahlil Gibran, copyright © 1923 by Kahlil Gibran and renewed 1951 by Administrators C.T.A. of Kahlil Gibran Estate and Mary G. Gibran; reprinted by permission of Alfred A. Knopf, Inc.

Tessa Sayle Agency Ltd for permission to quote from 'Immanence', a poem from the book *Immanence* by Evelyn Underhill. Dent, London, 1912.

Simon & Schuster for permission to quote from *Stay Alive All your Life* by Norman Vincent Peale, copyright © 1985, 1957, used by permission of the publisher, Prentice Hall, a division of Simon & Schuster, Englewood Cliffs, NJ.

PICTURE CREDITS

Title page: *Flowers,* Joyce Haddon; January: *Setting Out – A Frosty Morn,* R.G. (Fine Art Photographs); February: *Woodland Snowdrops,* Myles Birket Foster (Fine Art Photographs); March: *Spring Flowers,* Myles Birket Foster (Fine Art Photographs); *Sheep in a Landscape,* Joyce Haddon; April: *Picking Buttercups,* Helen Allingham (Fine Art Photographs); May: *Spring,* John Clayton Adams (Fine Art Photographs); June: *Wild Roses,* William Stephen Coleman (Fine Art Photographs); *Roses,* Joyce Haddon; July *Young Girl by a Garden Gate,* Mildred Butler (Fine Art Photographs); August: *On the Beach at Rottingdean,* Myles Birket Foster (Fine Art Photographs); *On the Sea Shore,* Joyce Haddon; September: *Harvesting,* John Clayton Adams (Fine Art Photographs); October *Collecting Firewood,* George Todd (Fine Art Photographs); November: *By the Fireside,* John Abercrombie (Fine Art Photographs); December: *A Christmas Recital,* Freidrich Ortlieb (Fine Art Photographs).